The Political Philosophy of AI

The Political Philosophy of AI

An Introduction

Mark Coeckelbergh

polity

First published in 2022 by Polity Press

Polity Press
65 Bridge Street
Cambridge CB2 1UR, UK

Polity Press
101 Station Landing
Suite 300
Medford, MA 02155, USA

ISBN-13: 978-1-5095-4853-8
ISBN-13: 978-1-5095-4854-5(pb)

A catalogue record for this book is available from the British Library.

Library of Congress Control Number: 2021941737

Typeset in 10.5 on 12pt Sabon
by Fakenham Prepress Solutions, Fakenham, Norfolk NR21 8NL
Printed and bound in Great Britain by CPI Group (UK) Ltd, Croydon

The publisher has used its best endeavours to ensure that the URLs for external websites referred to in this book are correct and active at the time of going to press. However, the publisher has no responsibility for the websites and can make no guarantee that a site will remain live or that the content is or will remain appropriate.

For further information on Polity, visit our website:
politybooks.com

Contents

Acknowledgments

I wish to thank my editor, Mary Savigar, for her support and for guiding this book project to its successful conclusion, Justin Dyer for his careful editing, and Zachary Storms for assisting with the organizational aspects linked to the submission of the manuscript. I also thank the anonymous reviewers for their comments, which helped me to polish the manuscript. I am especially grateful to Eugenia Stamboliev for assisting with the literature search for this book. Finally, I warmly thank my family and friends – nearby and distant – for their support during these two difficult years.

1

Introduction

"I guess the computer got it wrong": Josef K. in the 21st century

> Someone must have been telling tales about Josef K., for one morning, without having done anything wrong, he was arrested. (Kafka 2009, 5)

This is the first line of *The Trial* by Franz Kafka, originally published in 1925 and widely considered one of the most important novels of the 20th century. The protagonist of the story, Josef K., is arrested and prosecuted, but he does not know why. The reader is also left in the dark about this. Many explorations and encounters follow that only increase the opacity of it all, and after an unfair trial, Josef K. is executed with a butcher's knife, "like a dog" (165). The story has been interpreted in many ways. One political take is that it shows how oppressive institutions can be and that its descriptions do not only reflect the rising power of modern bureaucracy but also prefigure the horrors of the Nazi regime that took place a decade later: people were arrested without having done anything wrong and sent to camps, facing various forms of suffering and often death. As Adorno put it: Kafka offers a "prophecy of terror and torture that was fulfilled" (Adorno 1983, 259).

Unfortunately, Kafka's story is still relevant today. Not only because there are still opaque bureaucracies and oppressive regimes, which arrest people without justification and sometimes without trial, or because (as Arendt [1943] and Agamben [1998] already pointed out) refugees are often suffering a similar fate, but also because there is now a new way in which all this can happen, indeed *has* happened, even in a so-called "advanced" society: one that has to do with technology, in particular with artificial intelligence (AI).

On a Thursday afternoon in January 2020, Robert Julian-Borchak Williams received a call in his office from the Detroit Police Department: he was asked to come to the police station to be arrested. Since he hadn't done anything wrong, he didn't go. An hour later he was arrested on his front lawn, in front of his wife and children, and, according to the *New York Times*: "The police wouldn't say why" (Hill 2020). Later, in the interrogation room, detectives showed him an image from a surveillance video of a black man shoplifting from an upscale boutique and asked: "Is this you?" Mr. Williams, who was African American, responded: "No, this is not me. You think all black men look alike?" Only much later was he released, and in the end the prosecutor apologized.

What happened? The *New York Times* journalist and the experts she consulted suspect that "his case may be the first known account of an American being wrongfully arrested based on a flawed match from a facial recognition algorithm." The facial recognition system, using AI in the form of machine learning, is faulty and most likely also biased: it works better for white men than for other demographics. The system thus creates false positives, like in the case of Mr. Williams, and, combined with bad police work, this results in people being arrested for crimes they didn't commit. "I guess the computer got it wrong," one of the detectives said. In the 21st-century United States, Josef K. is black and is falsely accused by an algorithm, without explanation.

The moral of the story is not only that computers make mistakes, mistakes that can have severe consequences for particular people and their families; the use of AI can also worsen existing systemic injustices and inequalities, and in response to cases such as that of Mr. Williams, one could argue that all citizens should have a right to explanation when decisions are made about them. Moreover, this is just *one* of the many ways in which AI can have political significance and impact, sometimes intended but often unintended. This particular case raises questions concerning racism and (in)justice – two timely issues. But there is much more to say about the politics of AI and related technologies.

Rationale, aims, and approach of this book

While there is currently plenty of attention directed to *ethical* issues raised by AI and related technologies such as robotics and automation (Bartneck et al. 2021; Boddington 2017; Bostrom 2014; Coeckelbergh 2020; Dignum 2019; Dubber, Pasquale, and Das 2020; Gunkel 2018; Liao 2020; Lin, Abney, and Jenkins 2017; Nyholm 2020; Wallach and Allen 2009), there is very little work that approaches the topic from a *political-philosophical* angle. This is regrettable, since the topic lends itself perfectly well to such an investigation and leaves valuable intellectual resources from the political-philosophical tradition unused. From their side, most *political philosophers* have left the topic of the politics of AI untouched (exceptions are Benjamin 2019a; Binns 2018; Eubanks 2018; Zimmermann, Di Rosa, and Kim 2020), although in general there is a growing interest in the topic, for example in how algorithms and big data are used in ways that reinforce racism and various forms of inequality and injustice (e.g., Bartoletti 2020; Criado Perez 2019; Noble 2018; O'Neil 2016) and that extract and consume planetary resources (Crawford 2021).

Moreover, while in the current *political context* there is a lot of public attention directed to issues such as freedom, slavery, racism, colonialism, democracy, expertise, power, and climate, often these topics are discussed in a way that makes it seem as if they have little to do with technology and vice versa. AI and robotics are seen as technical subjects, and *if* a link to politics is made, technology is seen as a tool used for political manipulation or surveillance. Usually, the unintended effects remain unaddressed. On the other hand, *developers and scientists* working in the fields of AI, data science, and robotics are often willing to take ethical issues into account in their work, but are not aware of the complex political and societal problems these issues are connected to, let alone of the sophisticated political-philosophical discussions that could be held about the framing and addressing of these problems. Moreover, like most people not familiar with systematic thinking about technology and society, they tend to assume the view that technology itself is neutral and that everything depends on the humans developing and using it.

Questioning such a naïve conception of technology is the speciality of *philosophy of technology*, which in its contemporary form has advanced a non-instrumental understanding of technology: technology is not just a means to reach an end, but also shapes these ends (for an overview of some theories, see Coeckelbergh 2019a). However, when it comes to using philosophical frameworks and conceptual foundations for the normative evaluation of technology, philosophers of technology usually run to ethics (e.g., Gunkel 2014; Vallor 2016). Political philosophy is largely ignored. Only some philosophers make this connection: for example, in the 1980s and 1990s, Winner (1986) and Feenberg (1999), and today, Sattarov (2019) and Sætra (2020). More work is needed on the nexus between philosophy of technology and political philosophy.

This is an academic gap, but also a societal need. If we want to tackle some of the most pressing global and local issues of the 21st century such as climate change, global inequalities, aging, new forms of exclusion, war, authoritarianism, epidemics and pandemics, and so on, each of which is not only politically relevant but also related to technology in various ways, it is important to create a dialogue between thinking about politics and thinking about technology.

This book fills these gaps and responds to this rationale by

- connecting normative questions about AI and robotics to key discussions in political philosophy, using both the history of political philosophy and more recent work;
- addressing controversial issues that are at the center of current political attention, but now linking them to questions regarding AI and robotics;
- showing how this is not just an exercise in applied political philosophy but also leads to interesting insights into the often hidden and deeper political dimension of these contemporary technologies;

- demonstrating how the technologies of AI and robotics have both intended and unintended political effects, which can be helpfully discussed by using political philosophy;
- thereby making original contributions to both philosophy of technology and applied political philosophy.

The book thus uses political philosophy, alongside philosophy of technology and ethics, with the aims (1) to better understand normative issues raised by AI and robotics and (2) to shed light on pressing political issues and the way they are entangled with the use of these new technologies. I use the term "entangled" here to express the close connection between political issues and issues concerning AI. The idea is that the latter is *already* political. The guiding concept of this book is that AI is not just a technical matter or just about intelligence; it is not neutral in terms of politics and power. AI is *political through and through*. In each chapter, I will show and discuss that political dimension of AI.

Rather than staging a discussion about the politics of AI in general, I will approach this overall theme by zooming in on specific topics that figure in contemporary political philosophy. Each chapter will focus on a particular political-philosophical set of themes: freedom, manipulation, exploitation, and slavery; equality, justice, racism, sexism, and other forms of bias and discrimination; democracy, expertise, participation, and totalitarianism; power, disciplining, surveillance, and self-constitution; animals, the environment, and climate change in relation to posthumanism and transhumanism. Each theme will be discussed in the light of the intended and unintended effects of AI, data science, and related technologies such as robotics.

As the reader will notice, this division in terms of topics and concepts is to some extent artificial; it will become clear that there are many ways in which the concepts, and hence the topics and chapters, interlink and interact. For example, the principle of freedom may be in tension with the principle of equality, and it is impossible to talk about democracy and AI without talking about power. Some of these connections will be made explicit in the course of the book; others are left to the reader. But all chapters show how AI impacts these key political issues and how AI is political.

However, this book is not only about AI but also about

political-philosophical thinking itself. These discussions of the politics of AI will not only be exercises in applied philosophy – more specifically applied political philosophy – but will also feed back into the political-philosophical concepts themselves. They show how new technologies put our very notions of freedom, equality, democracy, power, and so on, into question. What do these political principles and political-philosophical concepts mean in the age of AI and robotics?

Structure of the book and overview of its chapters

The book is organized into seven chapters.

In chapter 2, I ask questions related to the political principle of freedom. What does freedom mean when AI offers new ways of making, manipulating, and influencing our decisions? How free are we when we do digital labour for large, powerful corporations? And does the replacement of workers by robots lead to the continuation of slavery thinking? The chapter is structured according to different conceptions of freedom. It discusses the possibilities offered by algorithmic decision-making and influencing by connecting to long-standing discussions about liberty in political philosophy (negative and positive liberty) and nudging theory. It points out how negative liberty can be taken away on the basis of an AI recommendation, questions how libertarian nudging by means of AI really is, and asks critical questions based on Hegel and Marx, showing how the meaning and use of robots risk remaining connected to a history and present of enslavement and capitalist exploitation. The chapter ends with a discussion of AI and freedom as political participation and freedom of speech, which is continued in chapter 4 on democracy.

Chapter 3 asks: what are the (usually unintended) political effects of AI and robotics in terms of equality and justice? Does the automation and digitalization enabled by robotics increase inequalities in society? Does automated decision-making by AI lead to unjust discrimination, sexism, and racism, as Benjamin (2019a), Noble (2018), and Criado Perez (2019) have argued, and, if so, why? Is the gendering of robots problematic, and how? What is the meaning of justice and fairness used in these discussions? This chapter puts the debates about automation and discrimination by AI and robotics in the context of classical political-philosophical discussions about (in)equality and (in)justice as fairness in the liberal-philosophical tradition (e.g., Rawls, Hayek), but also connects to Marxism, critical feminism, and anti-racist and anti-colonial thinking. It raises questions concerning the tension between conceptions of universal justice versus justice based on group identity and positive discrimination, and discusses issues regarding inter-generational justice and global justice. The chapter ends with the thesis that AI algorithms are never politically neutral.

In chapter 4, I discuss the impacts of AI on democracy. AI can be used to manipulate voters and elections. Does surveillance by AI destroy democracy? Does it serve capitalism, as Zuboff (2019) has argued? And are we on our way to a kind of "data fascism" and "data colonialism"? What do we mean by democracy, anyway? This chapter puts the discussions about democracy and AI in the context of democracy theory, discussions about the role of expertise in politics, and work on the conditions for totalitarianism. First, it shows that while it is easy to see how AI can threaten democracy, it is much harder to make explicit what kind of democracy we want and what the role of technology is and should be in democracy. The chapter outlines tensions between Platonic-technocratic conceptions of politics and ideals of participative and deliberative democracy (Dewey and Habermas), which in turn have their critics (Mouffe and Rancière). It connects this discussion to issues such as information bubbles, echo chambers, and AI-powered populism. Second, the chapter argues that the problem of totalitarianism through technology points to deeper and long-standing problems in modern society such as loneliness (Arendt) and lack of trust. Ethical discussions, insofar as they focus on harm to individuals, neglect this broader societal and historical dimension. The chapter ends by pointing to the danger of what Arendt (2006) called "the banality of evil" when AI is used as a tool for corporate manipulation and bureaucratic management of people.

Chapter 5 discusses AI and power. How can AI be used for disciplining and self-disciplining? How does it impact on knowledge and shift and shape existing power relations: between humans and machines but also between humans and even within humans? Who benefits from this? To raise these questions, the chapter connects back to discussions about democracy, surveillance, and surveillance capitalism, but also introduces Foucault's complex view of power that highlights the micro-mechanisms of power at the level of institutions, human relationships, and bodies. First, the chapter develops a conceptual framework with which to think about relations between power and AI. Then it draws on three theories of power in order to elaborate on some of these relations: Marxism and critical theory, Foucault and Butler, and a performance-oriented approach. This enables me to shed light on the seductions and manipulations of and by AI, the exploitation and self-exploitation that it produces and its capitalist context, and the history of data science in terms of marking, classifying, and surveilling people. But it also points to ways in which AI may empower people and – through social media – play a role in the constitution of self and subjectivity. Moreover, it is argued that, by seeing what AI and humans do here in terms of technoperformances, we can point to the increasingly leading and more-than-instrumental role that technology plays in organizing the ways we move, act, and feel. I show that these exercises of (techno)power always have an active and social dimension, which involves both AI and humans.

In chapter 6, I introduce questions concerning non-humans. Like most ethics of AI, classic political discussions are human-centered, but this can and has been questioned in at least two ways. First, are humans the only ones who count, politically? What are the consequences of AI for non-humans? And is AI a threat or an opportunity for dealing with climate change, or both? Second, can AI systems and robots themselves have political status, for example citizenship? Posthumanists question the traditional anthropocentric view of politics. Moreover, transhumanists have argued that humans will be superseded by superintelligent artificial agents. What are the political implications if a superintelligence takes over? Is this the end of human freedom, justice, and democracy? Opening up resources from animal rights and environmental theory (Singer, Cochrane, Garner, Rowlands, Donaldson and Kymlicka, Callicott, Rolston, Leopold, etc.), posthumanism (Haraway, Wolfe, Braidotti, Massumi, Latour, etc.), ethics of AI and robotics (Floridi, Bostrom, Gunkel, Coeckelbergh, etc.), and transhumanism (Bostrom, Kurzweil, Moravec, Hughes, etc.), this chapter explores conceptions of AI politics that go beyond the human. It argues that such a politics would require a rethinking of notions such as freedom, justice, and democracy to include non-humans, and would raise new questions for AI and robotics. The chapter ends with the claim that a non-anthropocentric politics of AI reshapes both terms of the human–AI relation: humans are not only de-powered and *em*powered by AI, but also give AI its power.

The concluding chapter summarizes the book and concludes that (1) the issues we currently care about in political and societal discussions such as freedom, racism, justice, and democracy take on a new urgency and relevance in the light of technological developments such as AI and robotics; and that (2) conceptualizing the politics of AI and robotics is not a matter of simply applying existing notions from political philosophy and political theory, but invites us to interrogate the very notions themselves (freedom, equality, justice, democracy, etc.) and to ask interesting questions about the nature and future of politics and about ourselves as humans. The chapter also argues that, given the close entanglement of technology with societal, environmental, and existential-psychological changes and transformations, political philosophy in the 21st century can no longer evade what Heidegger (1977) called "the question concerning technology." The chapter then outlines some further next steps that need to be taken in this domain. We need more philosophers working in this area and more research on the nexus of political philosophy/philosophy of technology, hopefully leading to a further "thinking together" (*zusammendenken*) of politics and technology. We also need more thinking about how to render the politics of AI more participatory, public, democratic, inclusive, and sensitive to global contexts and cultural differences. The book ends with the question: what *political technologies* do we need for shaping that future?

2

Freedom: Manipulation by AI and Robot Slavery

Introduction: Historical declarations of liberty and contemporary slavery

Freedom or liberty (I will use these terms interchangeably) is considered one of the most important political principles in liberal democracies, whose constitutions aim to protect basic liberties of citizens. For example, the First Amendment of the US Constitution, adopted in 1791 as part of the Bill of Rights, protects individual freedoms such as freedom of religion, freedom of speech, and freedom of assembly. Germany's constitution or Basic Law (*Grundgesetz*), adopted in 1949, states that the freedom of the person is inviolable (Article 2). Historically, the French Declaration of the Rights of Man and of the Citizen of 1789 is very influential. It is rooted in Enlightenment thinking (Rousseau and Montesquieu) and was developed at the time of the French Revolution in consultation with Thomas Jefferson: one of the founders of the United States and the principal author of the 1776 US Declaration of Independence, which already proclaimed in its preamble that "all men are created equal" and that they have "unalienable Rights," including "Life, Liberty and the pursuit of Happiness." Article I of the French Declaration says that "Men are born and remain free and equal in rights." While this Declaration still excluded women and did not forbid slavery, it was part of a history of declarations of rights and civil liberties that started in 1215 with Magna Carta (*Magna Carta Libertatum* or the great charter of freedoms) and ended with the Universal Declaration of Human Rights (UDHR), adopted by the United Nations General Assembly in December 1948, which states that "All human beings are born free and equal in dignity and rights" (Article 1) and that "No one shall be held in slavery or servitude" (Article 4) (UN 1948).

Yet in many countries in the world, people still suffer from, and protest against, oppressive and authoritarian regimes that threaten or violate their liberty. Often protest has lethal consequences: consider, for example, how political opposition is treated in contemporary Turkey, Belarus, Russia, China, and Myanmar. And while slavery is illegal, new forms of slavery continue today. The International Labour Organization estimates that globally there are more than 40 million people in some form of forced labor or forced sexual exploitation, for example in domestic work or in the sex industry (ILO 2017). It occurs within countries and via trafficking. Women and children are especially affected. It happens in North Korea, Eritrea, Burundi, the Central African Republic, Afghanistan, Pakistan, and Iran, but also persists in countries such as the US and the UK. According to the Global Slavery Index, in 2018 there were an estimated 403,000 people working under forced labor conditions in the US (Walk Free Foundation 2018, 180). Countries in the West also import goods and services that risk having involved modern slavery at the site of production.

But what does liberty mean, exactly, and what does political liberty mean in the light of developments in AI and robotics? To answer these questions, let us look at a number of threats to freedom, or, rather, threats to *different kinds of freedoms*. Let us examine some key conceptions of freedom developed by political philosophers: negative freedom, freedom as autonomy, freedom as self-realization and emancipation, freedom as political participation, and freedom of speech.

AI, surveillance, and law enforcement: Taking away negative freedom

As we have seen in the introduction, AI can be used in law enforcement. It can also be used in border policing and airport security. Across the world, facial recognition technology and other biometric technologies such as fingerprints and iris scans are being employed in airports and other border crossing sites. As well as incurring the risk of bias and discrimination (see the next chapter) and threats to privacy (UNCRI and INTERPOL 2019), this can lead to all kinds of interventions that infringe on a person's *freedom*, including arrest and imprisonment. If an error is made by the AI technology (e.g., miscategorizing a person, not recognizing a face), individuals may be falsely arrested, denied asylum, publicly accused, and so on. A "small" margin of error may impact thousands of travelers (Israel 2020). Similarly, so-called *predictive policing*, which uses machine learning to "predict" crime, may lead to unjustified liberty-depriving judicial decisions, in addition to (again) discrimination. More generally, it may lead to "Kafkaesque" situations: opaque processes of decision-making and arbitrary, unjustified, and unexplained decisions, significantly affecting the lives of defendants and threatening the rule of law (Radavoi 2020, 111–13; see also Hildebrandt 2015).

The kind of freedom that is at risk here is what political philosophers call "negative liberty." Berlin famously defined negative liberty as freedom from interference. It concerns the question: "What is the area within which the subject – a person or a group of persons – is or should be left to do or be what she is able to do or be, without interference from other persons?" (Berlin 1997, 194). Negative freedom is thus the absence of interference, coercion, or obstruction by others or the state. This is the kind of freedom that is at stake when AI is used to identify people who pose a security risk, who are said to have no right to migration or asylum, or who have committed a crime. The freedom that is threatened is a freedom of non-interference.

In the light of surveillance technologies, one could extend this conception of freedom to the freedom of not being at *risk* of interference. This negative freedom is at stake when AI technology is used for surveillance to keep people in a state of enslavement or exploitation. The technology creates invisible chains and ever-watching non-human eyes. The camera or the robot is always there. As has often been observed, this situation resembles what Bentham and, later, Foucault called the Panopticon: prisoners are watched, but they cannot see the watchers (see also chapter 5 on power). Physical restraint or direct supervision, as in earlier forms of imprisonment or slavery, is no longer necessary; it suffices that the technology is there to monitor people. It does not even have to function, technically speaking. Compare this with the speed camera: whether it actually functions or not, it already influences – in particular, *disciplines* – human behavior. And this is part of the very design of the camera. Knowing that you are being watched all the time, or could be watched all the time, is enough to discipline you. It is sufficient that there is a risk of interference; this creates the fear that one's negative freedom will be taken away. This can be used in prisons and camps, but also in work situations in order to monitor the performance of employees. Often surveillance is hidden. We do not see the algorithms, the data, and those who use these data. Bloom (2019) speaks, somewhat misleadingly, of "virtual power" because of this hidden aspect. But the power is real.

AI surveillance is not only used in law enforcement and by governments, or in corporate environments and work contexts; it is also employed in the private sphere. For example, on social media there is not only "vertical" surveillance (by the state and by the social media company) but also peer surveillance or "horizontal" surveillance: social media users watch each other, mediated by algorithms. And there is *sousveillance* (Mann, Nolan, and Wellman 2002): people use portable devices to record what is happening. This is problematic for various reasons, but one reason is that it threatens freedom. Here this could mean the negative freedom to have privacy, understood as freedom from interference in the personal sphere. Privacy is usually seen as a basic right in a liberal, that is, free society. But this may be in danger in a society in which we are asked to embrace a culture of sharing. As Véliz (2020) puts it: "Liberalism asks that nothing more should be subjected to public scrutiny than what is necessary to protect individuals and cultivate a wholesome collective life. A culture of exposure requires that everything be shared and subjected to public inspection" (110). Full transparency thus threatens liberal societies, and big tech plays an important role in this. Using social media, we voluntarily create digital dossiers about ourselves, with all kinds of personal and detailed information that we willingly share, without any governmental Big Brother forcing us to give it or having to do the painstaking work to acquire it in covert ways.

Instead, tech companies openly and shamelessly take the data. Platforms such as Facebook are an authoritarian regime's but also a capitalist's wet dream. People create dossiers and track *themselves*, for example for social purposes (meeting) but also health monitoring.

Moreover, such information can be and has been used against people for law enforcement. For example, based on analysis of data from her Fitbit device, an activity and health tracker, US police charged a woman with making a false report about rape (Kleeman 2015). Fitbit data were also used in a US murder case (BBC 2018). Data from social network sites and phones can be used for predictive policing, which may have consequences for personal liberty. Yet even if there are no threats to freedom from interference, the problem is also situated at the societal level and impacts different kinds of freedoms, such as freedom as autonomy (see the next section). As Solove (2004) puts it: "[I]t is a problem that implicates the type of society we are becoming, the way we think, our place in the larger social order, and our ability to exercise meaningful control over our lives" (35).

That being said, when it comes to threats to negative liberty by means of technology, the issue can get very physical. Robots can be used to physically restrain people, for example for security or law enforcement purposes, but also for "people's own good" and safety. Consider the situation when a young child or an elderly person with cognitive impairments risks crossing a dangerous road without watching or risks falling from a window: in such cases a machine could be used to restrain the person by, for example, preventing that person from leaving a room or leaving the house. This is a form of paternalism (more in the next section) that restricts negative liberty by means of surveillance followed by a physical form of interference. Sharkey and Sharkey (2012) even see in the use of robots to restrict the activities of the elderly "a slippery slope towards authoritarian robotics." Such a scenario concerning monitoring and restraining humans through AI and robotics technology seems more realistic than the distant, science-fiction scenario of superintelligent AI taking over power – which may also lead to taking away liberty.

Anyone using AI or robotics to restrict the negative liberty of people has to justify why it is necessary at all to violate such a basic kind of freedom. As Mill (1963) argued in the mid-19th century, when it comes to coercion, the burden of proof should be on those who contend for a restriction or prohibition, not on the people defending their negative liberty. In the case of privacy violations, law enforcement, or paternalistic restriction of movement, the onus is on the one who restricts to show that there is a considerable risk of harm (Mill) or that there is another principle (e.g., justice) that is more important than liberty – in general or in the particular case. And justifying such uses and interventions becomes even harder when the technology makes mistakes (the false match case in the introduction) or when the technology itself causes harm. For example, facial recognition may lead to unjustified arrest and imprisonment, or a robot may cause injury when and while restraining someone. Furthermore, beyond utilitarian and, more generally, consequentialist frameworks, one could emphasize rights to liberty from a deontological point of view, for example the rights to liberty enshrined in national and international declarations.

Yet considering these cases when the technology has (unintended) harmful effects, it becomes clear that there is more at stake than liberty alone. There are tensions and trade-offs between liberty and other political principles and values. Negative freedom is very important, but there may also be other political and ethical principles that are very important and that (should) play a role in a particular case. It is not always clear which principle should prevail. For example, whereas it may be crystal clear that it is justified to restrain the negative freedom of a small child in order to prevent a particular harm (e.g., falling out of a window), it gets far less clear that such restrictions to freedom are justified in the case of an older adult with a dementia condition or in the case of someone who is said to live "illegally" in a particular country. And is it justified to restrict the negative liberty of one person (e.g., by means of imprisonment) in order to protect the negative liberty and other political rights of other persons?

Application of Mill's harm principle is also notoriously difficult. What, exactly, constitutes harm in a particular case, who defines which harm is done to whom, and whose harm is more important? And what counts as a restriction of negative liberty anyway? Consider, for example, the obligation to wear a mask in specific places during the COVID-19 pandemic, which has led to controversies about precisely these questions: who needs more protection from (the risk of) harm, and is wearing a mask taking away negative liberty? These questions are also relevant in the case of use of AI. For example, even if a particular AI technology were to work without errors, is an airport security screening procedure that involves scanning and facial recognition itself an infringement of my liberty not to be interfered with? Is a hand search such an infringement, and if so, is it more of an infringement than a scanner? Does a facial recognition error itself constitute a harm, or does that depend on the potentially harmful actions of the security personnel? And if all this is justified by referring to the risk of terrorism, does this small-probability (but high-impact) risk justify the measures that interfere with my negative liberty when I cross a border and my exposure to the new risks that the technology creates, including the risk that my negative liberty is taken away due to a technological error?

AI and the steering of human behavior: Circumventing human autonomy

But if these issues concern negative freedom, what is positive freedom? There are various ways to define positive freedom, but one central meaning defined by Berlin has to do with autonomy or self-governance. Here the question is whether your choice is really your choice rather than that of someone else. Berlin (1997) writes:

> The "positive" sense of the word "liberty" derives from the wish on the part of the individual to be his own master. I wish my life and decisions to depend on myself, not on external forces of whatever kind. [...] I wish, above all, to be conscious of myself as a thinking, willing, active being, bearing responsibility for my choices and able to explain them by reference to my own ideas and purposes. (203)

This kind of freedom is contrasted not with interference in the sense of imprisonment or obstruction, but rather with paternalism: someone else decides what is best for you. Berlin argues that authoritarian rulers distinguish between a higher self and a lower self, claim to know what your higher self really wants, and then oppress people in the name of that higher self. This kind of freedom is not about absence of external restraint or physical disciplining; it is an interference in your psychology of desire and choice.

What does this have to do with AI? To understand this, consider the possibility of nudging: changing the choice environment with the aim to alter people's behavior. The concept of nudging exploits the psychology of human decision-making, in particular biases in human-decision making. Thaler and Sunstein (2009) propose nudging as a solution to the problem that people cannot be trusted to make rational decisions and instead use heuristics and bias to decide. They argue that we should influence people's decision-making by changing their choice environment in the desirable direction. Instead of coercing people, we alter their "choice architecture" (6). For example, instead of banning junk food, fruit is offered at eye level and in a prominent place in the supermarket. This intervention thus operates subconsciously; it targets the part of the brain we share with lizards (20). Now AI could be, and has been, used for this kind of nudging, for example when Amazon makes recommendations for products it claims I should want to buy. Likewise, Spotify seems to claim to know me better than I do when it recommends particular music. Such recommender systems nudge since they do not restrict my choice of books or music, but influence my buying, reading, and listening behavior in the direction suggested by the algorithm. And the same technology can be used or encouraged by governments, for example to steer behavior in a more environmentally friendly direction.

These kinds of interventions do not take away people's freedom of choice or freedom of action. There is no coercion. This is why Thaler and Sunstein call nudging a form of "libertarian paternalism" (5). It is not done against people's will. It therefore differs from classic paternalism, for example as defined by Dworkin (2020): "the interference of a state or an individual with another person, against their will, and defended or motivated by a claim that the person interfered with will be better off or protected from harm." Whereas classic paternalism clearly violates negative freedom, nudging steers people's choices in what is taken to be their best interests without restricting their liberty in the way Dworkin describes it. Or to use Berlin's terminology: nudging does not violate negative liberty since there is no external restraint. For example, a government that wants to promote the public health of its citizens may require that tobacco firms put a warning on cigarette packages that smoking kills or have supermarkets remove them from particular prominent places such as the checkout. This policy does not ban cigarettes, but requires that producers and retailers put nudges in place that are meant to influence the choices people make. Similarly, a recommender system driven by AI does not force you to buy a specific book or listen to a particular song, but may influence your behavior.

Yet while this is not a threat to negative freedom since no one is forced to do something or to decide something, nudging by AI is a threat to positive freedom. By working on people's subconscious psychology, it manipulates them without respecting them as rational persons who wish to set their own goals and make their own choices. Forms of subconscious manipulation such as advertising and propaganda are not new. But nudging pretends to be libertarian and, accelerated by AI, is likely to have a pervasive influence. Nudging can be done by corporations but also by the state, for example in order to achieve a better society. But with Berlin (1997) one could argue that violations of positive liberty in the name of social reform are degrading: "To manipulate men, to propel them towards goals which you – the social reformer – see, but they may not, is to deny their human essence, to treat them as objects without wills of their own, and therefore to degrade them" (209). According to Berlin, paternalism is "an insult to myself as a human being" (228) because it fails to respect me as an autonomous being who wants to make my own choices and shape my own life. And this charge also seems applicable to the so-called "libertarian" paternalism of nudging, in which case people are not even aware that their choices are influenced, for example in the supermarket.

This renders nudging by means of AI at the very least highly suspect and – like all violations of negative liberty – *prima facie* unjustified (unjustified unless proven otherwise). Someone who still wants to use the technology in this way has to argue that there is a more important principle and good than positive liberty. For example, one could argue that a person's health and life are more important than respecting his or her autonomy, or that the survival of humanity and other species is more important than the positive liberty of people being ignorant of their effects on climate or unwilling to contribute to solving that problem. But while presumably infringements of positive liberty are seen as less controversial than violations of negative liberty, it is important to understand what is at stake here: the risk of treating people as objects that can and must be manipulated for their own good or the good of society (e.g., nudging against obesity), disregarding their capacities for autonomous choice and rational decision-making, and treating them as means to ends (e.g., means to reach climate goals), ends which others (e.g., the government, green reformers) conceived independently of them. When and why do the ends (e.g., the good goals) justify the means, justify such degradations, if at all? And who decides the goals?

To understand people as mainly or basically irrational and not open to argumentation is also a very pessimistic view of human nature and society, which is in line with the political philosophy of Hobbes. According to Hobbes (1996), writing in mid-17th-century England, a state of nature would be a nasty condition in which there would be only competition and violence. To avoid this, he argued, a political authority, a Leviathan, was needed to bring order. Similarly, libertarian paternalism is pessimistic about people's own capacity to build a social order that is good for themselves and for society. That social order has to be imposed from above by means of manipulation, for example by using AI. Other political philosophers, such as Rousseau in the 18th century and Dewey and Habermas in the 20th, instead hold a more optimistic view of human nature and believe in democratic forms of politics according to which people are seen as capable of voluntarily committing to the common good, rationally deliberating, and arguing towards a consensus. According to such views, humans should neither be controlled (restrictions to negative freedom, despotism) nor manipulated (restrictions to positive freedom, paternalism); they are very well capable of restraining themselves, thinking rationally and beyond their own self-interest, and discussing with each other about what is good for society. In this view, society is not a collection of atomized individuals but a republic of citizens directed towards achieving the common good. Like others defending philosophical *republicanism*, Rousseau (1997) looked back to the ancient Greek city states and thought that the common good could be achieved through active citizenship and participation, and that citizens should submit to a "general will," forming a community of equals. While in Rousseau's case there is a notorious problem

with his view that one should be *forced to be free*, that is, forced
"to consult [one's] reason before listening to [one's] inclinations"
(53) and submit to the general will, he rejected despotism and
generally his view is optimistic about human nature: the state of
nature is good and already social. He also agreed with ancient
philosophers like Plato and Aristotle that freedom as autonomy
is both attainable and desirable at the personal level through use
of reason and restraint of the passions (a view we can also find
in virtue ethics). It remains an open question what the role of AI
could be in the light of such ideals. In chapter 4 I will further
outline different views on the possibility of democracy and
related ideals, and in chapter 5 on power I will say more about
AI and self-constitution.

Threats to self-realization and emancipation: Exploitation by means of AI and the problem with robot slaves

Another threat to freedom comes not from interfering with
one's negative liberty or from nudging but from violations of
a different, more relational kind of freedom: oppression and
exploitation by others through labor in a capitalist context,
or even (openly) through forcing others into a relationship of
slavery and domination. While this may involve restrictions to
negative freedom of individuals – of course I cannot do what
I want when I'm a slave and *do not even get into a position in
which what I want matters* since I am not viewed as a political
subject in the first place – and while oppression may also be
combined with violations of positive freedom (exploitation),
these phenomena also raise problems concerning *self-realization,
self-development, and emancipation*, link to problems of justice
and equality (see also the next chapter), and concern the quality
of human *social relationships*, the value of labor and its relation
to nature and freedom, and the question of how to structure
society. The kind of freedom threatened here is relational in the
sense that it is not about the management of inner desires or
about seeing others as external threats, but about building better
social relationships and societies.

For this conception of freedom, Hegel and Marx are sources
of inspiration. According to Hegel, transformation of nature

through work leads to self-consciousness and freedom. This goes back to the famous master–slave dialectic in the *Phenomenology of Spirit* (1977; originally 1807): whereas the master is dependent on his desires, the slave attains the consciousness of freedom through work. Marx borrowed this idea that labor leads to freedom. In his hands, freedom is no longer an individualist notion that has to do with freedom from restraint or psychological autonomy, like Berlin's negative and positive freedom; it is a more social, materialist, and historical concept. For Hegel and Marx, freedom is grounded in social interaction; it is not opposed to dependency. Labor and tools extend our freedom. This freedom has a history, which is also a social and political history and (one could add) a history of technology. Marx thought that by means of technology, we can transform nature and at the same time create ourselves. By doing labor, we develop ourselves and exercise our human capacities.

However, Marx also argued that under capitalism, this becomes impossible, since workers are alienated and exploited. Instead of emancipating and realizing themselves, workers become unfree because they become alienated from their product, from others, and ultimately from themselves. In his *Economic and Philosophic Manuscripts of 1844*, Marx (1977, 68–9) wrote that workers themselves become commodities and servants of the objects they produce and of those who appropriate those products. Instead of affirming themselves, workers mortify their body and ruin their mind, rendering the labor forced rather than free (71). They become estranged from themselves as their labor becomes "an activity performed in the service, under the dominion, the coercion, and the yoke of another man" (76). Under such conditions, technology does not lead to freedom but becomes an instrument of alienation. Communism, by contrast, Marx argues, will be the realization of freedom, understood as (again) self-realization and the association of free people.

What does this notion of freedom mean for AI and robotics?

First, AI and its owners need data. As users of social media and other apps that require our data, we are the workers who produce these data. Fuchs (2014) has argued that social media and search engines such as Google are not liberating but colonized by capitalism. We are doing free labor for social media companies and their clients (advertisers): we produce a commodity (data), which is sold to corporations. This is a form of exploitation.

Capitalism requires that we continuously work and consume, including our use of electronic devices to produce data. Most of us live in a 24/7 capitalist economy; the only "freedom" we can find is in sleep (Crary 2014; Rhee 2018, 49). Even when we are in bed, the phone demands our attention. Moreover, the devices we use are often produced under "slave-like conditions" (Fuchs 2014, 120) as they rely on the hard labor of those who produce them and who extract the minerals from which they are built. AI services also rely on low-paid workers who clean and tag data, train models, and so on (Stark, Greene, and Hoffmann 2021, 271). However, in the light of Marx's analysis in terms of freedom as self-realization, the problem when I use social media is not only that I'm doing free labor and that others are exploited to enable my social media pleasures (which can be analyzed on the basis of the political economy approach in Marx's *Capital* (1990; originally 1867): the value created by workers in excess of their own labor costs is appropriated by the capitalist), but also that it is not leading to my self-development and self-realization and hence freedom. Instead, I become myself an object: a collection of data (see also chapter 5).

Second, robots are a technology that is often used for automation, and this has effects that can be described by using the Marxian conception of human freedom. For a start, robots come in the form of machines that contribute to the alienation described by Marx: workers become a mere part of the machine and lose the chance to realize themselves through work. This already happened in industrial production; soon it may happen in the service industry, for example in retail or restaurants (e.g. in Japan). In addition, as Marx describes, the use of machines leads not only to bad working conditions and the physical and mental deterioration of workers, but also to unemployment. The use of robots to replace human workers creates a class of unemployed people who have only their labor to sell (the proletariat). This not only is bad for those who lose their jobs, but also lowers the wages for those who are still employed (or keeps the wages as low as legally allowed). Moreover, some see their work devalued: it could as well be done by a robot (Atanasoski and Vora 2019, 25). The result is unfreedom in the sense of exploitation and lack of opportunities for self-realization.

While today it is widely accepted that robotics and AI will likely lead to consequences for employment (Ford 2015), authors disagree about the projected speed and extent of these developments. Economists such as Stiglitz predict a serious disruption, and warn about the human cost of the transition. For example, Korinek and Stiglitz (2019) predict a major disruption of labor markets, leading to greater income inequality, more unemployment, and a more divided society, unless individuals are fully insured against these effects and the right forms of redistribution are in place (such as those characteristic of European social welfare democracies). Moreover, the socio-economic consequences of AI may differ between so-called advanced societies and the Global South (Stark, Greene, and Hoffmann 2021). From a Marxian point of view, these issues can be conceptualized in terms of equality, but also freedom as self-realization. Low wages and unemployment are not only bad because they threaten the physical existence of people; they also render people less politically free because they cannot realize themselves.

Against such views, some have argued that machines will liberate humankind from dirty, heavy, dangerous, or boring work, freeing up time for leisure and self-realization. Unemployment due to replacement by machines is then welcomed as a step on the road to liberty. Instead of seeing labor as a way to freedom, as Hegel and Marx did, this adopts the ancient Aristotelian idea that freedom is about freeing yourself up from the necessities of life. According to Aristotle, occupying oneself with the necessities of life is something for slaves, not for free people. Marxians, however, would not only disagree with this view of labor but also point out that Aristotle's society was based on slavery: the political elite could only enjoy their privileged lives by exploiting others. A defender of what is often called "the leisure society" could reply that technology would end human enslavement and that the consequences of unemployment could be addressed by a system of social security, for example by means of universal basic income which would guarantee that no one, including those unemployed because of the machines, would be poor. But Marxians may argue that AI capitalism may actually no longer need humans at all: in this scenario, capital gains "freedom from a humanity that becomes a biological barrier to accumulation" (Dyer-Witheford, Kjøsen, and Steinhoff 2019, 149).

These issues raise further philosophical questions. From a Hegelian perspective, for example, one could worry that if all humans were to become masters (masters of machines), they would lack opportunities for self-realization and be delivered to their desires, which could then be manipulated and exploited by capitalists. The masters would become in turn exploited consumers: a new, different kind of slaves. To some extent this seems already the case today. As Marcuse (2002) has argued, consumer society brings its new forms of domination. Not only are the masters dependent on the machines they control; as consumers, they are dominated once again. Moreover, keeping in mind the master–slave dialectic, once they replace slaves by machines, the masters (in this scenario: all of us) no longer have the opportunity to be recognized at all, since they cannot possibly receive recognition from machines as these lack the self-consciousness necessary. Thus, if Hegel is right that the master is dependent on the slave for recognition, then the problem is that here the master receives no recognition at all. In other words, in a society of human masters and robot slaves, the master-consumers are not free at all and, worse, do not even have a chance to become free. As slave-consumers, they are dominated and exploited under capitalism. As masters over machines, they do not receive recognition. And as I have stressed in earlier work on this topic, they also become highly dependent on the technology and thus vulnerable (Coeckelbergh 2015a).

But why think in terms of masters and slaves at all? On the one hand, replacing human slaves or workers by robots can be seen as liberating, from a Marxian and even from a more general Enlightenment point of view: humans are no longer inserted into these exploitative social relationships. On the other hand, thinking in terms of servants or slaves, even in the case of robots, seems altogether problematic. Is it OK to have robot slaves? Is it OK to *think* about society in terms of masters and slaves? And it's not just about thinking. If we replace human slaves by machines, the structure of our society is then still one based on slavery, albeit one in which the slaves are artificial: a cyber version of ancient Rome or ancient Greek city states. There is no violation of Article 4 of the UDHR, since that article applies only to humans (it is about *human* rights) and the robots are not slaves in the human sense since they lack consciousness, sentience, intentionality, and so on. But the setup where robots take the place of human servants or slaves still reflects master-slave thinking and a hierarchical and "exploitative" master–slave society. What is wrong is the kind of social relationships and the kind of society these technologies help to maintain. (The next chapter offers a further argument.)

Now one could try to bypass these problems by arguing that this is not about liberty, but about something else. The problem with oppression, exploitation, and slavery is not *liberty* (at least if one understands liberty in the individualist and more formal way articulated in the previous sections) but *justice* or *equality*. According to this view, the problem is not so much that AI and robotics threaten freedom, but rather that we live in a society that is fundamentally unequal or unjust, and that we risk maintaining or worsening these inequalities and injustice by means of AI and robotics. For example, if we "liberate" workers by replacing them with machines, but do not change the structure of our present societies (by means of universal basic income or other measures), then we will likely create more inequality and injustice. We need more public discussion about what kind of society we have and want. Political-philosophical concepts and theories such as equality and justice can help with this. For instance, like current social security systems, universal basic income reflects a particular conception of distributive justice and justice as fairness. But which one? In the next chapter, I will outline some conceptions of justice.

However, it is also interesting to discuss such issues from the angle of freedom. For example, in *Real Freedom for All* (1995), Van Parijs defends an unconditional basic income for all based on notions of justice, equality, and *freedom*. He understands freedom not as a formal right to do what one wants (the usual libertarian notion of freedom, e.g. in Hayek), but as the actual capacity to do so. Freedom is thus defined in terms of opportunity. People with more advantages (e.g., more access to assets) are more free than others in terms of opportunity. Unconditional income would make the least advantaged more free in this opportunity sense, while respecting the formal freedom of others, thus creating freedom for all. Furthermore, everyone could use these opportunities in accordance with their own conception of the good. Liberals should be neutral with respect to people's conceptions of the good (within legal limits). To take up one of Van Parijs's own examples: if people want to spend a lot of their time surfing, this is fine; they have the opportunity to do so. He calls this "real libertarianism." On the basis of this view, one could argue that, when machines take over human jobs, universal basic income is a way not only of creating more justice and equality, but also of respecting and promoting the liberty of all. People could work or surf or both; they would have real freedom in the sense of freedom of opportunity.

However, as the discussion about universal basic income shows, there is much more to say about the political and societal dimension of AI and robotics in terms that go beyond liberty. We also need to talk about equality and justice, and about how AI and robotics can perpetuate or aggravate existing forms of bias and discrimination (see the next chapter).

Who decides about AI? Freedom as participation, AI in elections, and freedom of speech

Another meaning of freedom is *political participation*. Again this idea has ancient, more specifically Aristotelian roots. As Arendt explains in *The Human Condition* (1958), freedom for the ancients was not liberal freedom of choice, but political action, which she distinguishes from other activities in the *vita activa* (labor and work). According to philosophical republicanism, one can only exercise one's freedom by means of political participation. While for the ancient Greeks this freedom was reserved for an elite and in fact rested on the slavery of those who labored and hence were denied that political freedom, the idea of freedom as political participation is important in the history of modern political philosophy and has inspired some key interpretations and ideals of democracy (see chapter 4). As I already indicated earlier in this chapter, a well-known modern expression of the idea of freedom as participation in political decision-making comes from Rousseau, who argued already before Kant that freedom means giving a rule to oneself. This self-rule can be interpreted as individual autonomy (see the section above on nudging), but Rousseau also gave self-rule a political meaning: if citizens make their own rules, they are truly free and not delivered to the tyranny of others. However controversial Rousseau's further thoughts on the general will may be, the idea that political participation is and should be part of liberal democracy has stuck and has influenced the way many of us think about democracy today.

What does the conception of freedom as self-participation mean for the question of freedom regarding AI and robotics? Here are some normative arguments one could make about the politics of AI and robotics based on this conception.

First, decisions about technologies and their use are often not taken by citizens but by governments and corporations: by politicians, managers, investors, and developers of the technology. This is also the case for AI and robotics, which are often developed in military contexts (government funding) and in tech companies. Based on the ideal of freedom as political participation, one could criticize this and demand that citizens participate in public discussion and political decisions about AI and robotics. While one can also make this argument by relying on the principle of democracy, from the perspective of philosophical republicanism it can be justified on the basis of freedom: if freedom means political participation and political self-rule, then the current situation in which citizens have little or no influence on the use and future of technology is effectively keeping them in a state of unfreedom and despotism. Citizens lack self-rule with regard to these decisions. In the name of freedom as participation, one should request more democratic decision-making concerning our technological future.

Moreover, beyond demanding changes to the usual political institutions, one could ask that innovation processes themselves take into account citizens as stakeholders and their values. During the past decade, there have been arguments for responsible innovation and value-sensitive design (Stilgoe, Owen, and Macnaghten 2013; van den Hoven 2013; von Schomberg 2011): the idea is that societal actors are included in innovation processes and that ethical values are taken into account at the design stage. But this is not only a question of ethical responsibility: based on the ideal of freedom as participation, one could also see it as a *political* imperative. Freedom should not only be about my freedom of choice as a user or consumer of technology – taking the technology I use as given – but also be about my freedom to participate in decisions and innovation processes concerning the technologies I use. Exercising this freedom is especially important since, as philosophers of technology continue to stress, technologies have unintended effects and shape our lives, societies, and the persons we are. If freedom as self-rule is an important political principle, then with regard to technologies such as AI, it is important not only that I gain personal autonomy over my use of technology (and responsibility) as a user and consumer, but also that I, as a citizen, have a say in, and political responsibility for, decisions concerning the technology. If this kind of freedom as participation is lacking, then the future of AI and robotics – which is also *my* future – remains in the hands of technocratic politicians and despotic CEOs, owners, and investors.

Second, however, even as participants in politics we might be manipulated by means of AI. AI plays an increasing role in election campaigns and in political life in general. For example, evidence suggests that AI was used to manipulate citizens in Donald Trump's 2016 presidential campaign (Detrow 2018): the data science company Cambridge Analytica targeted individual voters with advertising based on profiling of their psychology, using data about their behavior on social media, consumption patterns, and relationships. And bots on social media such as Facebook and Twitter, disguised as human accounts, can be used to spread misinformation and fake news to specific demographic groups (Polonski 2017). This is a problem for democracy (see chapter 4) but also for freedom. It relates back to threats to freedom as autonomy and to the issue of surveillance, but also influences freedom as political participation.

But the problem with regard to manipulation is not just about political manipulation in a narrow sense: that is, manipulation for political purposes in contexts that are usually defined as political. When we use our smart devices everywhere, at work but also at home, we are increasingly operating in smart environments in which automated agents shape our choice environments. Hildebrandt (2015) sees this in analogy to the autonomic nervous system that governs our heart rate: similar to the autonomic nervous system adjusting our internal environment (our body), an autonomic computer system can now adjust our external environments "in order to do what it infers to be necessary or desirable for our own well-being." And all this happens without our conscious knowledge, just as we cannot know how exactly our vital functions are governed (55). This is a problem for freedom as autonomy and for society as a whole, insofar as "the social environment stops being formed through mutual expectations between people and becomes driven exclusively by the goals of data-driven manipulation" (Couldry and Mejias 2019,

182). But it also makes us think about what kind of political participation we want and need. How can we (re)gain more control over what happens to us and our environments technologically speaking? How can we gain the self-rule proposed by philosophical republicanism and Enlightenment thinking?

In chapter 4, I will say more about democracy as participation, but with regard to freedom, one could argue that one condition for freedom as political participation is education. Rousseau would not defend a political system such as ours in which political participation is decoupled from education; instead, and like Plato, he proposed moral education for citizens. For Rousseau, this is the only way we can realize the ideal of freedom as political participation. He would balk at the thought that the only thing citizens need to do is to vote every four or five years and that for the rest of the time they are left to do what they want, finding themselves in the hands of social media. He and other Enlightenment thinkers would also be appalled by the idea that citizens are a kind of consumers in a "self-service politics" and e-government in which the public administration is "customer-oriented" (Eriksson 2012, 691) or even co-producers of "public services" (687) – although the latter is certainly participative and gives citizens a more active role (691). Instead, like Plato, Rousseau thought that education should make people less self-interested, more compassionate, and less dependent on others, leading to moral dignity and respect and, as Dent (2005, 150) puts it, "the enactment of their full humanity in relation to one another." This moral and political education would then lead citizens to obey the general will in the sense that they would "do just what one would want to do as a moral being" (151). This ideal of political liberty as moral liberty based on education is threatened by a public sphere dominated by manipulation and misinformation, and AI can play a role in creating and maintaining such a sphere.

This leads us to another important liberty-relevant question in this area: should social media be more heavily regulated or regulate themselves, in order to create a better-quality public discussion and political participation at the cost of some negative freedom? Or is negative freedom, in the form of freedom of opinion and *freedom of speech* understood as the freedom to say what we want, more important than freedom as political participation and political action? Is the spreading of misinformation and hate a form of political participation and action at all? Is it acceptable since it respects negative freedom (freedom of speech), or is it the opposite of freedom since it may lead to totalitarianism (and hence lack of negative freedom) and the very corruption of politics and freedom as participation? Drawing on Aristotle and Rousseau, one could support the latter view, criticize liberal views (or at least their libertarian interpretations), and argue that freedom of speech does not include the freedom to say things that aim at destroying democracy, and that citizens should be educated to become better moral beings and participate in politics in a way that realizes their humanity. Whereas the first argument is very much established as a justification to limit freedom of speech in our current democracies, the second – moral education and political participation of citizens – is much more controversial. It would require regulation of the public sphere mediated by AI and other digital technologies, alongside substantial reforms in education and political institutions.

Restrictions to freedom of speech can be imposed by humans but also by AI. Digital social media platforms such as Twitter and even traditional media (e.g., online discussion forums of newspapers) already use AI for so-called "content moderation," which may involve automatic detection of potentially problematic content and automatic removal or demotion of that content. This can be used to block opinions that are seen as problematic or to remove misinformation and fake news (e.g., in the form of text or videos) that is used to politically manipulate audiences. In response to this use of AI, one could ask how accurate this evaluation is (in comparison with human evaluation) and whether the human evaluation is correct. There are also concerns that when human judgment is missing, this can give free rein to the use of AI for spreading misinformation, and that automating editorial decisions raises problems concerning accountability (Helberg et al. 2019).

But what, exactly, is missing? This question relates to the larger discussion concerning human judgment versus "judgment" by AI, which we can approach now by using discussions about *political* judgment. For example, according to Arendt (1968, interpreting Kant's aesthetic theory), political judgment has to do with a "*sensus communis*," or common sense, with having a world in common (sharing a world), and with use of the imagination to visit others' standpoints. She also refers to Aristotle's notion of *phronesis*, often understood to mean practical wisdom. This notion is known in virtue ethics, which focuses on the moral character and habits of persons and which has been used in thinking about robotics (e.g., Coeckelbergh 2021; Sparrow 2021), but in Arendt's work it also plays a political role. According to her, political judgment requires deliberation and imagination. Perhaps political judgment also includes an affective component, as Aavitsland (2019), influenced by Arendt, has argued – a claim that taps into a long-standing discussion about the role of rationality and emotions in politics. How could AI ever gain such a capacity for political judgment, given that, lacking consciousness and not being part of any "world" in that sense, it does not have any subjectivity, let alone inter-subjectivity, imagination, emotions, and so on? On the other hand, how good are humans at political judgment? Clearly, they often do not manage to exercise this kind of common sense, political imagination, and judgment, and do not get further than defending private interests. Moreover, those who – contra Arendt – hold a rationalist and naturalist notion of judgment may be tempted to argue that AI could do *better* than humans and offer a more "objective" judgment, free from emotions and bias. Some transhumanists discuss scenarios in which such an AI takes over power from humans, suggesting that this would be a good next step in the history of intelligence. But is objective or non-biased judgment possible at all? AI can, after all, also sometimes be biased – if not always. I will return to this question in the next chapter. And of course, like humans, AI can make errors: are we willing to accept this, in politics but also, for example, in a medical context (e.g., diagnosis, decisions about vaccination) or on the road (self-driving cars)? In any case, it is one thing to say that in some contexts AI can help *humans* to judge, by showing patterns in data and by offering recommendations and predictions based on calculation of probabilities; it is another to claim that what AI does constitutes making a judgment.

Yet in the light of the theme of this chapter, the main question to be discussed here concerns freedom: does content moderation by AI constitute damage to freedom of expression and is it justified at all? There are many warnings about this. Llansó (2020) has argued that, "regardless of advances in machine learning, filtering mandates are a threat to freedom of expression" and therefore to human rights. For example, several human rights advocates have called attention to the impact of AI, and at the level of the UN, a special rapporteur on freedom of expression has applied human rights law to evaluate the freedom of expression impact of AI used to moderate and curate content on digital platforms (UN 2018). The report makes a link to Article 19 of the UDHR. As well as drawing on the principle of free speech in the narrow sense of freedom of expression, one could argue that people have a right to be informed and a right to discuss. For example, UNESCO claims to promote the "free flow of ideas by word and image" (MacKinnon et al. 2014, 7).

Free discussion and exchange of ideas is especially important in a liberal democracy. Using political philosophy, one could argue with Mill that taking away freedom of speech risks stifling intellectual debate. In *On Liberty* (1978; originally 1859), Mill defended free expression of opinions on the ground that we otherwise end up with "intellectual pacification" (31) instead of minds that dare to push arguments to their logical limits. However, for Mill, freedom of opinion is not absolute, in the sense that people should be prevented from doing harm to others (the famous harm principle). In the liberal anglophone tradition, this is usually interpreted as harm to individual rights. For Mill, it's about not harming other individuals, and ultimately about maximizing their happiness. In the tradition of philosophical republicanism, however, the point is not that harm may be done to individuals. The problem is that hate speech, manipulation, and misinformation endanger the freedom of political partici-pation and political self-realization, the moral dignity of persons, and the common good. The harm that is being done is thus harm to the possibility of politics itself. And this philosophical republicanism seems compatible with at least one aspect of Mill's argument: the point of having freedom of expression is not expression as such, but political *argumentation* and *intellectual* debate. *This* is the freedom that should be respected. If we allow free speech, we should do so for the sake of respecting the dignity of persons and (we can add from a republican perspective) for the sake of promoting discussion that should lead to the common good and further realization of humanity.

According to Mill, discussion should lead to the truth. He argues that free speech is necessary for the sake of finding the truth through debate. Truth is valuable, and people might be wrong. Everyone is fallible. A free market of ideas increases the chance that truth can emerge and that dogmatic beliefs are challenged (Warburton 2009). Manipulation, misinformation, and anti-democratic propaganda, however, do not lead to these goals. They neither lead to a good political debate (the kind of political participation we want, according to Mill), nor support the goals of liberal Enlightenment and republican moral and political progress. If the use of AI leads to a public sphere in which reaching these goals becomes very difficult, then AI should either not be used in this area or be regulated in such a way that it supports, rather than corrupts, these political ideals.

However, if one wants to have such regulation, it remains difficult to specify who should regulate whom, and what liberty safeguards need to be in place. There is considerable discussion about the role of social media. On the one hand, it can be seen as undemocratic that big tech, in the form of companies such as Facebook and Twitter, decides who should be censored and when; more generally, it has been questioned why they have so much power. For example, one could ask why such platforms, infrastructures, and publishers need to be in private hands at all given their important role in today's democracy. As they dominate the media landscape and overpower public broadcasting services (originally set up to support democracy by means of education) and traditional media in general, they already play a significant political role. From this perspective, regulation is the least one could do. On the other hand, if government takes up the role of censor, is this justified, and what precise criteria should it use? Democratic governments routinely impose restrictions on free speech, but as philosophers we must question both the legitimacy of this role and the criteria used. And what if the government is taken over by an anti-democratic regime? If we let freedom of speech erode now, this will make it only easier for authoritarian regimes to destroy democracy.

Note also that traditional media such as newspapers and TV, at least the more or less independent, high-quality media, already had to deal with the problem of finding a balance between freedom of speech and moderation in order to enable a good discussion. Yet both in the case of private social media companies such as Twitter and established traditional newspapers, the *that*, *why*, *how*, and *who* of this moderation and censorship are not entirely transparent: we often do not know which voices are not heard, how that decision was justified (if at all), what procedures were followed (if at all), and who the moderators and censors were. Furthermore, we see that today national news media increasingly use automatic content moderation – just like Facebook and Twitter. This raises similar problems with regard to freedom of speech, alongside problems of fairness. While today most people seem to think that there is no absolute freedom of speech and *de facto* accept some moderation, serious issues remain, both in terms of freedom and in terms of other values and principles.

For example, contemporary critical theory has criticized the classical liberal-philosophical link between freedom of speech and negative freedom as freedom from interference for neglecting structural inequality, power, racism, and capitalism (see also the next chapter). Titley (2020) has analyzed how free speech is mobilized in far-right politics to spread racist ideas, and how superficial conceptions of free speech neglect structural inequalities between different speakers. Alongside the phenomenon of fake news, this helps to explain why in the current political context in the US, many liberals demand that companies like Facebook and Twitter impose more regulation and restriction of speech, for example hate speech, racist ideas, and misinformation, and see appeals to free speech as *a priori* problematic. In response, one could argue that the principle of free speech as such is not problematic, but that these problems show that we need a different and richer conception of it, especially in the age of digital communication: a conception that is more inclusive, truth-promoting, pluralist, and critical and takes into account lessons from contemporary political thinking while still retaining some aspects of Mill's vision, such as the belief in free intellectual debate. We then need to further discuss what free speech means in the age of automated journalism, AI censorship, and fake news – including fake videos and other products of AI.

Other politically relevant notions of freedom and other values

There are more notions of freedom that are impacted by AI. For example, transhumanists (see chapter 6) such as Bostrom, Sorgner, and Sandberg have proposed adding "morphological freedom" to the traditional individual liberal rights. Here the idea is that through advanced technologies – AI, but also nanotechnology, biotechnology, and so on – we will be able to refashion the human form beyond current biological limitations and control our own morphology (Roden 2015). This could be understood as a freedom at the level of humanity as a whole, but also as an individual freedom. For example, Sandberg (2013) has argued that the right to modify one's body is essential to any future democratic society and that it therefore should be seen as a basic right. One could make a similar argument for the right to modify one's mind, for example with the help of AI. Here it is not so much a traditional conception of freedom that has to be revisited and rediscussed in the light of new technological developments; rather, new technologies give us a new kind of freedom, which we did not previously have. Note, however, that such a freedom remains very close to the classic liberal notion of freedom as autonomy (positive freedom) and especially non-interference (negative freedom): the idea is that I, not others, decide what I do with my life, body, and mind.

To conclude, Marx and contemporary critical theory, but also philosophical republicanism inspired by Aristotelian philosophy, challenge the classical liberal and contemporary libertarian idea that freedom is mainly about non-interference and separation from others and about personal autonomy defined in a (merely) psychological way. Instead, they defend more relational and political conceptions of freedom, according to which we can only become truly free and emancipated if we realize ourselves as political beings and become part of a political community of equals that achieves self-rule, and that creates the conditions for this equality, inclusion, and participation. This approach enables us to ask the question of what the role of AI (and its human users) is, and can be, in hindering or facilitating the realization of such a conception of liberty and politics and its conditions. Moreover, each of these directions of thinking in its own way questions the steering and organization of society as a whole, rather than focusing on harm to individuals as such. While, in spite of their misuse, freedom from interference and the exercise of internal personal autonomy remain important principles and values in today's liberal democracies, the mentioned philosophies offer an interesting alternative framework with which to discuss what kind of political freedoms are afforded or threatened by AI and robotics, and indeed what kind of political freedoms and society we want.

Yet freedom is not the only thing that matters in the politics of AI. As I already suggested, freedom is also related to other important political values, principles, and concepts such as democracy, power, justice, and equality. For example, according to Tocqueville (2000), writing in the 1830s, there are trade-offs and fundamental tensions between liberty and equality; he warned about too much equality in the form of the tyranny of the majority. By contrast, Rousseau sees compatibility: his ideal of political freedom is based on the moral and political equality of citizens and requires some degree of socio-economic equality. In contemporary political-philosophical and economic thought, libertarians such as Nozick, Hayek, Berlin, and Friedman follow the trade-off view and think that liberty needs to be protected, whereas thinkers such as Habermas, Piketty, and Sen believe that too much inequality endangers democracy, which needs *both* freedom and equality (Giebler and Merkel 2016). The next chapter focuses on the principles of equality and justice and discusses their relevance to the politics of AI.

3

Equality and Justice: Bias and Discrimination by AI

Introduction: Bias and discrimination as a focus for raising problems concerning equality and justice

Digital technologies and media impact not only freedom, but also equality and justice. Van Dijk (2020) argues that network technology, while rendering production and distribution more effective and efficient, also leads to increasing inequalities: "Globally, it supports a tendency for the combined and uneven development of countries [...]. Locally, it helps to create dual economies of parts directly linked to the global information infrastructure and parts that are not" (336). This divergence in economic development creates societies with different "speeds" of development. Some people and countries benefit more from these technologies and media than others; this criticism can also be applied to AI. And as noted in the previous chapter, AI implemented in robotics may create unemployment and hence more inequality. Developments towards more automation have been in progress since at least the end of the 18th century. AI enables a next step in this automation revolution, which creates benefits for the few (the owners of AI tech and robots) and the risk of unemployment for the many. This is a problem not only for freedom and emancipation, but also for inequality. As we have seen, economists such as Stiglitz warn against greater income inequality and social division: AI impacts society as a whole. Unless measures are taken to reduce these effects – for example Piketty and colleagues have proposed high taxes above a certain (high) threshold (Piketty, Saez, and Stantcheva 2011); others have proposed universal basic income – high inequality and corresponding issues such as poverty will be the result.

One problem that is often related to AI specifically and that raises issues concerning equality and justice is bias. Like all technologies, AI has consequences that are not intended by its developers. One of these is that AI, in the form of machine learning, may introduce, maintain, and aggravate bias and thereby disadvantage and discriminate against specific individuals or groups, for instance against people defined in terms of race or gender. The bias can arise in various ways: there might be bias in the training data, in the algorithm, in the data the algorithm is applied to, and in the teams that program the technology.

A well-known case is that of the COMPAS algorithm, a risk assessment algorithm that was used in the US by the state of Wisconsin to decide about probation: the computer program predicts the risk of recidivism (tendency to reoffend). A study (Larson et al. 2016) found that COMPAS ascribed a higher risk of recidivism to black defendants than is actually the case, whereas white defendants were predicted to have a lower risk than is actually the case. Presumably trained on data of past decisions, the algorithm thus reproduced historical human bias and even increased it. Furthermore, Eubanks (2018) argues that information technology such as AI and "the new data regime" have a bad impact on economic equality and justice (8–9) since they often do not benefit poor and working-class people or empower them, but instead make things more difficult for them. The new technologies are used for manipulation, surveillance, and punishment of the poor and disadvantaged, for example in the form of automated decision-making about eligibility for benefits and its consequences, thus leading to a "digital poorhouse" (12). By means of automated decision-making and predictive analysis of data, the poor are managed, moralized, and even punished: "The digital poorhouse deters the poor from accessing public resources; polices their labor, spending, sexuality, and parenting; tries to predict their future behavior; and punishes and criminalizes those who do not comply with its dictates" (16). As well as undermining freedom, Eubanks argues, this creates and maintains inequality. Some people – the poor – are seen as having less economic or political value. Such problems come in addition to inequalities of access and use with regard to online information in general (the so-called digital divide). For example, less access leads to "fewer political, economic, and social opportunities" (Segev 2010, 8), which can also be framed as an issue of bias. Eubanks's (2018) analysis additionally shows that the use of digital technologies is associated with specific cultures, in this case a culture in the US with "punitive, moralistic views of poverty" (16). Implemented in the use of AI by governments, this contributes to the perpetuation of biases.

But problems of inequality and unfairness with regard to AI and data science also occur outside state institutions such as the juridical system, policing, and social welfare management. Consider, for example, a bank that has to decide about giving a loan: it may automate this decision by outsourcing it to an algorithm, which calculates the financial risk based on the applicant's financial and employment history but also information such as his or her postcode and statistical information about previous applicants. If there is a statistical correlation between having a particular postcode and not paying back loans, then someone living in that area may be denied a loan not based on an assessment of his or her individual risk, but on the basis of the patterns found by the algorithm. If the individual risk is low, this seems unfair. Moreover, the algorithm may reproduce the unconscious biases from bank managers who made previous decisions, for example a bias against people of color. Responding to the case of automated credit scoring, Benjamin (2019b, 182) warns of "'the scored society,' in which being scored in some way is part of the design of inequality"; those who have lower scores are punished. Or, to take a (non-standard) example from the gender domain: is it just that an algorithm decides that since a young male driver statistically has a higher car accident risk based on a correlation between gender and accidents, every young male driver has to pay more for his car insurance merely because he is male, even if the risk may be low for a particular individual? And sometimes data sets are also incomplete. For example, if an AI program is trained on datasets that lack sufficient data on women, in particular women of color, disabled women, and working-class women, then this could be seen as a shocking case of bias and gender inequality, as Criado Perez (2019) has argued.

Even something that is very mundane for most of us, like the use of AI-based search engines, can be problematic. Noble (2018) argues that search engines like Google reinforce racism and sexism, and that this should be seen as "algorithmic oppression" (1), which originates in decisions made by human beings and controlled by corporations. She claims that algorithms and classification systems are "embedded within" (13), and impact, social relations, including local and global racial power relations. She points out that corporations make money from racism and sexism, and draws attention to how African Americans are impacted in terms of identity, inequality, and injustice. For example, Google's search algorithm used to auto-tag African Americans as "apes" and linked Michelle Obama with the term "ape." Such cases are not only insulting and offensive; according to Noble, they also "demonstrate how racism and sexism are part of the architecture and language of technology" (9). The point is not that programmers intend to encode this bias. The problem is that they (and the users of the algorithms) assume that algorithms and data are neutral, whereas various forms of bias may be embedded in them. Noble warns against seeing technological processes as decontextualized and apolitical, a view which fits a conception of society in which individuals make their own choices in the free market (166).

Thus, the problem is not just that a particular AI algorithm is biased in a specific case and has particular consequences (e.g., political influence via journalists, who also use search engines such as Google; see Puschmann 2018); rather the main problem is that these technologies interact with, and support, existing hierarchical structures in society and the problematic conceptions and ideologies that fuel them. While users are not aware of it, these technologies support particular social, political, and commercial logics and frame the world in a particular way (Cotter and Reisdorf 2020). Like offline classification systems, which reflect the most powerful discourses in society (Noble 2018, 140), AI can thus lead to marginalization of ideas and the discrimination and oppression of people. More: via its scope and speed, it can dramatically amplify these. Noble shows that, like other digital technologies, AI is "implicated" in struggles for "social, political, and economic equality" (167) in a context of already existing and sometimes increasing social equality and injustice, and also in a context where some discourses have more power than others and represent oppressed people in particular ways by those who have more power (141).

Because of such tensions and struggles, public debates about AI in relation to bias, discrimination, racism, justice, fairness, gender discrimination, (in)equality, slavery, colonialism, oppression, and so on, often tap into, or soon become, highly polarized and ideological debates in particular contexts (e.g., debates about racism in the US). Furthermore, although computer scientists and tech firms have focused on technical definitions of bias and fairness, this is necessary but insufficient to address all the socio-technical problems (Stark, Greene, and Hoffmann 2021, 260–1). As noted, researchers such as Noble, Eubanks, and Benjamin have rightly pointed to this wider scope of problems of bias and discrimination.

Yet as philosophers, we must ask what is meant by the normative concepts used in these public discussions, technical practices, and popular literatures on bias in AI. For instance, we must ask what justice or equality means, since this shapes answers to the questions with regard to cases involving AI. Is something wrong in this particular case and, if it is wrong, then *why* exactly is it wrong, and what can and should be done about it and with what *aim*? In order to justify our opinions, construe good arguments, and have better discussions about biased AI, we (not just philosophers but also citizens, developers of technology, politicians, etc.) must examine concepts and arguments. This chapter shows that some notions and discussions from political philosophy, in particular, can be very helpful for this purpose.

First, I will provide an overview of standard anglophone political-philosophical discussions about equality and justice to shed light on what may be wrong with bias and discrimination by means of AI. I will ask what kind of equality and justice is at stake here and what kind of equality and justice we want. I ask the reader to consider different conceptions of equality and justice. Then I turn to two criticisms of liberal-philosophical thinking about these matters. Marxists and proponents of a politics of identity argue for a shift from individualist, univer-salist, and formal, abstract thinking towards class, group, or identity-based thinking (e.g., about race and gender). They also pay more attention to discrimination in the concrete lives of the disadvantaged and the historical background of that discrimination: colonialism, slavery, patriarchy, abuse, a history of hegemonic and capitalist social relations. In both cases, my purpose is not to offer an overview of the political-philosophical discussion as such, but to show what it implies for thinking about bias and discrimination in and by AI and robotics.

Why is bias wrong (1)? Equality and justice in standard anglophone liberal political philosophy

When AI is said to be biased, usually inexplicit assumptions are made about why it is biased and what is wrong with that. Philosophers can articulate and discuss the arguments. One type of argument is based on *equality*: if a recommendation or decision based on AI is biased, we could frame this as a case of treating people unequally. However, in political philosophy, there are substantial disagreements about what equality means. One conception of equality is *equality of opportunity*. In the universalist liberal "blind" conception of equality, this can be expressed as: people should have equality of opportunity, regardless of their socio-economic background, gender, ethnic background, and so on.

What does that mean in the context of AI? Imagine that an AI algorithm is used to select job applicants. Two criteria for success will very likely be education and relevant work experience: applicants who score higher on these will have a higher chance of getting a hire recommendation by the algorithm. The algorithm thus discriminates against people who have less education and relevant work experience. But this will usually not be called "discrimination" or "bias," since it is assumed that equality of opportunity is respected here in the sense that all applicants have had the opportunity to acquire the right kind of education and the relevant job experience and to apply for the job, regardless of criteria such as socio-economic background and gender. The algorithm is "blind" to these characteristics.

However, some philosophers question this conception of equality of opportunity: they argue that in practice some people (e.g., people with a worse socio-economic background) have had less chance to acquire the relevant educational background and experience. Real equality of opportunity, according to these critics, would mean that we create the conditions for these less advantaged people to have an equal chance to get the desired education and work experience. If this does not happen, the algorithm will discriminate against them and its decision can be called biased because of this chance inequality. If these critics adhere to a universalist liberal "blind" conception of equality, they will demand that all people get equal opportunities, regardless of where they come from, how they look, and so on. If AI – in spite of good intentions, perhaps – does not help to achieve this, it is biased and this bias needs to be fixed. Starting from a non-blind conception (see below), one could then demand more educational and job opportunities for the disadvantaged. One could also argue that as long as this is not the case, the algorithm would need to decide in a way that positively discriminates in favor of people from these (class) backgrounds, this gender, and so on. These are all different justifications for why AI may threaten equality, understood in terms of opportunities.

These arguments already point to two different conceptions of equality: one that is based on class or identity (see the next section) and one that is based on equality at the point of outcomes (here, jobs) rather than opportunities. People who want the algorithm to positively discriminate in favor of these specific classes or groups have a particular outcome in mind: a particular distribution with regard to the candidates selected (e.g., 50 percent female candidates) and in the end a society in which jobs are more equally distributed and historical inequalities are ended. AI could then help to bring about this outcome. This is no longer equality of opportunity but *equality of outcome*. But what does equality of outcome mean, and what should the distribution look like? Does it mean that everyone should have the same, that everyone should have a minimum, or should only great inequality be avoided? Moreover, as Dworkin (2011, 347) asks: is equality a value in itself?

In anglophone political philosophy, equality is not a very popular concept. Many classic introductions to political philosophy do not even have chapters on the theme (an exception is Swift 2019). A more common way of expressing bias and why it is wrong relies on the concept of justice, in particular *justice as fairness* (Rawls 1971; 2001) and *distributive justice*. It is typically said that the bias created by the algorithm is not *fair*.

But what does justice as fairness mean? And if anything needs to be redistributed at all, what counts as a fair distribution? Here, too, there are different conceptions. Consider again the example of the hiring AI. Suppose that the hiring AI, as well as taking into account criteria such as education and work experience, figures out that postcode is a statistically relevant category: imagine that there is a correlation between success in finding a job and living in a (socio-economically) "good," rich neighborhood. The result could be that, everything else being equal (e.g., all applicants have the same level of education), an applicant from a "bad," poor neighborhood has a lower chance of being selected by the algorithm. This seems unfair. But what, exactly, is unfair, and why?

First, one could say that it is unfair because while there is a statistical correlation, there is no causal one: while many people living in that neighborhood in fact have a less high chance of getting a job (due to other factors that are in play such as lack of a good education), the particular person in question does not and should not have a lower chance just because he or she belongs to this statistical category (having postcode x) and given that he or she actually does have a good education and does well on the other indicators. The person is treated unfairly because the decision is based on a criterion that is irrelevant in this particular case. Second, however, one could also wonder if it is fair that many other people in that neighborhood, who actually have received a worse education, have less relevant work experience, and so on, have less chance of getting a job. Why do we, as a society, allow such big differences in this respect? The problem could again be put in terms of equality of opportunity. But it could also be framed as being a matter of justice as fairness: the distribution of education, the distribution of chances of getting jobs, and the actual distribution of jobs are unfair. The next question then is: why, exactly, are these not fair, and what would be the just distribution?

According to one conception of justice as fairness, an *egalitarian* and *redistributive* one, what is needed is that everyone gets the same. Here this means: the social policy and the AI algorithm make sure that everyone gets equal opportunities to get a job or that everyone gets a job (in which case one would not need the selection algorithm in the first place). While this is a popular way of dealing with distributive justice at the kitchen table or among friends (e.g., when a cake needs to be distributed), it tends to be less favored when it comes to politics, job hire, and so on. Many people seem to think that when it comes to society, a completely equal distribution is not fair and merit should matter, that talented people deserve more, and (surprisingly, in my view) that inherited wealth and support do not pose problems of justice at all. Nozick (1974), for example, thinks that people can do what they want with what they own: they are entitled to it as long as it is acquired by means of voluntary transfers. He defends a minimal state which protects rights to life, liberty, property, and contract, and rejects the concept of redistributive justice.

But since talent and inherited money are not under the control of individuals and are a matter of luck, one could argue that they should not play a role for justice and that inequalities based upon them are unfair. A *meritocratic* conception of justice would restrict the success selection to factors that have to do with what people actually do, for example work hard to get a job. A fair algorithm would, then, be one that takes merit into account. However, this is also problematic, since outward criteria such as degrees and other outcomes do not necessarily tell us much about how hard a person has worked to obtain that result. How do we know what the person in our example has done to get the degree? For example, it could be that it was easy for an applicant to acquire his or her degree given his or her educational and social background. And how do we know the merit of people who live in a "bad" neighborhood? When we consider their background and see this in terms of bad results (here, lack of a degree), we may think that they have not done much to improve their position, whereas in reality this may not be true at all and they would therefore deserve much more than they get on the basis of a so-called meritocratic conception. Justice understood in terms of merit may be fair, but not so easy to realize.

Yet even if one rejects justice as absolute distributive equality or justice based on merit, there are other conceptions of justice. One is that it is just if everyone gets a minimum of a particular good – here, the chance to get a job. According to this *sufficitarian* conception of justice (e.g., Frankfurt 2000; Nussbaum 2000), we need to create a threshold. In such a society, people who live in rich neighborhoods would still have a higher chance of being picked up by the algorithm. But the person living in the poor neighborhood would, regardless of other factors, have *a minimum* chance of getting a job. The correlation between living in a particular neighborhood and getting a job would still be there but its relevance in the decision process would be weakened. This would be the case either because there is a different policy that brings about this change before or after the algorithm does its work, or because the algorithm is tweaked in such a way that it gives a minimum chance to everyone (a threshold for success), with other factors having the potential to increase that chance but it being impossible to go below the threshold. Alternatively, everyone may get a minimum of working hours (and hence income) or a minimum of money.

According to a *prioritarian* conception of justice, however, this would still not be fair. People from good neighborhoods will still have a much higher chance of getting the jobs, and when they have a job, their jobs will be full-time and much better paid. What is needed, according to prioritarians, is giving priority to the most disadvantaged. Here this could mean a policy that focuses on giving disadvantaged people jobs (regardless of other criteria) or on significantly increasing job chances for people who are already disadvantaged: for example, by means of an algorithm that increases the job chances of people living in a poor neighborhood, even if they score less on relevant factors such as education and work experience.

A famous political-philosophical justification for a prioritarian position, which also responds to the observation that talent is a matter of luck and builds in equality of opportunity, has been provided by Rawls. In his *A Theory of Justice* (1971), he used the thought of experiment of the so-called "veil of ignorance" in the "original position" (12). Imagine that you do not know if you will be born with talents, if you will have rich or poor parents, if you will have equal opportunities, if you will live in a "good" or "bad" neighborhood, and so on, and do not know which social position you will have in society, then what kind of principles of justice (and hence what kind of society) would you choose? Rawls thought that people would come up with two principles: one that gives equal liberties to all, and one that arranges social inequalities in such a way that they are to the greatest benefit of the least advantaged and create equality of opportunity. Inequalities are fine if they maximize the position of the worst-off. This is called the difference principle (60).

According to these Rawlsian principles, the problem with the biased algorithm that selects on the basis of postcodes is not that its recommendation reflects an unequal distribution of socio-economic resources in society or a society in which some people fall below a minimum threshold, but that it mirrors and reveals a society in which there is no equality of opportunity and in which inequalities do not maximize the position of the worst-off. If these principles would have been implemented in policy, then presumably we would not have such a high correlation between postcode and the chance to get a job. The other people living in the area would have had more chances to get a job and would not be in such a bad social position. Therefore, the algorithm would have only found a weak correlation, and postcode would not have played such an important role in its recommendation. The situation of the well-educated person with a good background but living in a poor area full of people having social positions which differ hugely from his or her own would not exist, or the problem would be at least less pronounced, and therefore this specific problem of discrimination by the algorithm would not arise. Moreover, even if the current situation is highly unjust, one could change the algorithm in such a way that it maximized the position of those who are worst-off: a positive discrimination that would change the actual situation according to Rawls's difference principle. One could call this "positive discrimination by design," as a specific form of "fairness by design."

Note that this form of positive discrimination would require that programmers and designers are aware of potential bias in the first place, especially *unintended* bias. More generally, they would have to be aware that even if no discrimination or other politically relevant consequences are intended, design choices may have such consequences, for example in terms of justice and equality. There is still much work to be done on creating awareness about potential political consequences, on recognizing bias, and more generally on implementing political and ethical values in design. For example, recognizing bias may be difficult when there are no explicit references to criteria such as gender, race, and so on, in the training data (Djeffal 2019, 269). And when the problem is not recognized, there can be no solution, including in terms of positive discrimination. Technical work on algorithmic fairness can help with this: it tries to identify, measure, and improve fairness when using AI algorithms (e.g., Pessach and Shmueli 2020). Combined with the right kind of legal framework, this can lead to what Hacker (2018, 35) calls "equal treatment by design." But as we have seen, equality is just one way of framing the issues. Furthermore, design can also be used to positively discriminate. In that case, the aim and definition of algorithmic fairness are not that the results are independent of variables such as gender, ethnicity, and so on, in order to avoid a negative bias, but instead that a positive bias is created towards one or more of such variables, thus correcting for historic or existing unfairness.

As we are about to see, however, usually measures of positive discrimination are proposed not by those working in the liberal-philosophical tradition but by those who criticize that tradition, or at least criticize its universalism.

Why is bias wrong (2)? Class and identity theories as criticisms of universalist liberal thinking

Marxian theory has criticized liberal-philosophical accounts of justice and equality for focusing on formal and abstract principles while not touching the basic capitalist structure of society, according to which formally free individuals voluntarily make contracts (see also Nozick again), but which actually creates and maintains a division and hierarchy between two classes: one which owns the means of production and another which gets exploited by the former under capitalist conditions. Instead of imagining hypothetical positions and contracts, we should look at the material and historical conditions that create injustice and inequality, and change them. Instead of keeping apart questions regarding production and distribution, we should change the way we organize production. In this sense, a communist society would be beyond justice (Nielsen 1989), at least if justice is understood as redistributive justice. Instead of first having capitalist production and then redistributing according to principles of justice, as liberal theory has it, we should abolish capitalism itself. Instead of evaluating society from a disinterested standpoint, we should defend the interests of the class that is exploited. Instead of talking about principles of justice applied to individuals and aggregates of individuals, we should focus on class and class struggle.

From this perspective, then, biased algorithms and the societies to which they are applied are not unjust, unfair, and so on, because they fail to apply and embody an abstract idea of justice or equality, but rather because they help to create and sustain a socio-economic system, capitalism, which creates hierarchical social relations between two classes: those who own and those who do not own the means of production. The problems set up by liberal theory are framed within a capitalist world. Consider again the loan example or the hiring example: both cases take place within a capitalist social and economic structure, in which it is in the interest of capitalists to keep a class of people in debt and in precarious socio-economic positions open to exploitation. The bias, then, is not just in the algorithm or in the particular social situation; within capitalism itself there is a bias and a dynamic that advantages some (the capitalists as owners of the means of production) and disadvantages others (the working class, which becomes the proletariat). AI is used as a means of exploitation and robots are used to replace workers and create a proletariat of unemployed people, which makes it easier to exploit those who still have jobs. The problem is not AI but what we could call "AI capitalism" – to use a more general term than Zuboff's (2019) "surveillance capitalism" and to highlight the role of AI. Unless this fundamental problem is addressed, there will be neither justice nor equality. One could tweak the algorithms to benefit the disadvantaged, but ultimately these are just symptomatic treatments. The real problem is that AI and robotics are used within a capitalist system, which uses these technologies not for the emancipation of the people but for the sole benefit of making the capitalists even richer than they already are. Moreover, the belief that the free market will eliminate algorithmic discrimination over time is "ill-founded," since those who employ the algorithms have no incentive to minimize bias (Hacker 2018, 7). In the example, the bank and the company that hires people operate within the capitalist logic and do not believe it is their job to reduce discrimination. If this is not changed, symptomatic treatments will not help much. Nor will there even be an incentive on the part of the capitalists to really change the technologies and their use, since that is not in their interest.

Seen from this perspective, it is then important for workers and others to resist the system and struggle against AI-driven capitalism. However, one problem is that they often do not know that AI is being used, let alone that it categorizes and discriminates. Its workings and its contribution to the creation of biases are hidden. Furthermore, the impact of AI capitalism on workers is not equal. Some jobs are more precarious than others. To some extent, all jobs have become more precarious. Azmanova (2020, 105) speaks of "precarity capitalism," claiming that "economic and social insecurity has become a core feature of our societies," which leads to anxiety and stress (Moore 2018). Even those who have skilled and well-paid jobs are not secure. Yet some jobs are clearly more precarious than others, and some workers and selves are more quantified than others (see chapter 5). This also means that the psychological consequences of contemporary capitalism are distributed unequally: some form "anxious selves who have internalised the imperative to perform" (Moore 2018, 21) more than others; some fear replacement by machines (15) more than others. And whereas low-status workers are highly exposed to surveillance without a possibility to opt out, high-status workers are more protected, although their data are also exploited (Couldry and Mejias 2019, 191). Everyone is vulnerable, existentially, socio-economically, and psychologically, but some are more vulnerable than others. Furthermore, there are cultural differences in how AI is perceived: some cultures have more positive attitudes than others towards AI (and technology in general). (This also impacts challenges related to regulating AI, especially at the global level – I will return to this in my conclusion.) Taken together, this implies that some will be more motivated to revolt against AI capitalism than others, if they are aware of the technology-related problems at all. This calls into question the Marxian ideal of a broad alliance between workers under the umbrella of one class (consciousness).

Yet social change is not just about people and their actions and labor; technology, including AI, is deeply part of the system. In their book *Inhuman Power* (2019), Dyer-Witheford, Kjøsen, and Steinhoff – some of the most prominent Marxian analysts of technology – argue that AI should be seen as the culmination of the alienation of workers under capitalism: AI represents the power of autonomous capital, leading to commodification and exploitation. This can be framed as a problem of freedom (see the previous chapter) but also as a problem of capitalism creating deep inequality and injustice. It may also be a problem for other political values. For example, as Frankfurt (2015) argues, economic inequality is also a problem for democracy: "Those who are much better off have a serious advantage over those who are less affluent – an advantage that they may tend to exploit in pursuing inappropriate influence over electoral and regulatory processes" (6).

Liberals such as Frankfurt argue that inequality "cannot itself be our most essential ambition" (5). Yet for Marxians, the problem is not just the effects on democracy but the inequality itself, as linked to capitalist exploitation. Moreover, whereas (left) liberal thinkers would then proceed to demand redistribution, without saying anything about the means of production (here, AI), for Marxians this is a key point. For example, Dyer-Witheford suggests that social change would require changing the entire socio-economic system as well as the technology, since AI and capital are so entangled. Paradoxically, then, if the proletariat wants to take action against capital, it will have to use AI but at the same time also be against it (Dyer-Witheford 2015, 167). Perhaps one could understand this in the light of what Marcuse (2002) wrote about Marx's view that a reorganization of the means of production is needed. According to Marx, production should be organized by the immediate producers. But when technology "becomes the medium of control and cohesion in a political universe which incorporates the laboring classes," Marcuse argues, we need "a change in the technological structure itself" (25).

This suggests that technology itself needs to be changed. However, most Marxians focus on the *ownership* of the means of production, without questioning the technologies themselves. According to Fuchs (2020), a truly just society must be commons-based, which means that information should be a common good instead of a commodity and that there should be common control of the conditions of communication. Capital tries to subsume commons. Fuchs proposes that instead workers should "obtain the collective control of the means of communication as means of economic production" (310) and that platforms such as Facebook should be civil-society-based cooperatives (311). Fuchs puts this "antagonism between information as a common good and as a commodity" in terms of justice and equality: "If the commodity form implies inequality, then a truly fair, democratic and just society must be a commons-based society.

For the communication system, this means that communication systems as commons correspond to the essence of humanity, society and democracy" (28). Similarly, one could argue that AI and data, understood as communication technologies and information, are means of production in a Marxian sense and should be held in common instead of controlled by capital. Moreover, one could question the technological optimism and technological determinism of transhumanist visions of AI (Fuchs calls them "posthumanist"), which seem to assume "that society and humanity radically change because of the rise of new technologies" (21) and that this change is necessarily good. Fuchs warns that this neglects the importance of class and capitalism in society (21) and leads to the replacement of people by robots and a concentration of power instead of democracy and equality (82). Furthermore, it has been argued that to think that new information and communication technologies are necessarily progressive is to deny the "antagonistic conditions" of their emergence and "their embeddedness within the brutalities of global capitalism" (Dean 2009, 41).

Currently very popular in the US, an alternative approach that is critical of the classical liberal-philosophical approach to justice and equality focuses not on socio-economic categories but on categories that have to do with identity, such as race and gender. Sometimes this approach is called "identity politics." While this phrase itself is politically very laden and controversial, it refers to "a wide range of political activity and theorizing found in the shared experiences of injustice of members of certain social groups" (Heyes 2020). If identity politics uses political principles such as freedom, justice, and equality, it is to secure these principles for specific groups, defined in terms of their identity and history. Whereas theorists from the liberal-philosophical tradition take a universalist stance (e.g., demand justice for all or equality for all), people who adhere to identity politics thinking argue that this has not been sufficient to stop the marginalization or oppression of particular social groups such as women, people of color, LGBT+ people, indigenous people, disabled people, and so on. To address these problems, they put (group) identity in the center of political attention. One could say that they lift the Rawlsian veil of ignorance. Instead of engaging in a distant thought experiment about abstract individuals and societies that are composed of these individuals, they ask us to look at concrete realities and histories of injustice against (people of) particular groups. Like Marxians, they want to change the social structures that generate injustice and look at concrete historical realities rather than appeal to abstract universalist notions. However, they demand this not so much because a particular socio-economic class is disadvantaged and because capitalism is problematic, but rather because particular identity-defined groups are currently and historically disadvantaged. Moreover, if paired with a politics of difference, justice is demanded, but with the aim not of inclusion in universal humankind *regardless* of identities and differences, but of respecting these identities and differences themselves. This also means recognizing particular groups and people belonging to these groups, rather than talking about a universal "we." As Fukuyama (2006) explains the idea: since Hegel, politics has been linked to recognition, but now "universal recognition based on a shared humanity is not enough, particularly on the part of groups that have been discriminated against in the past. Hence modern identity politics revolves around demands for recognition of group identities" (9). These identities are historically situated and locally constructed, and often emerge against particular forms of oppression and injustice.

Today this form of politics is popular on the liberal left. What Dyer-Witheford calls the "post-Marxist" position dismisses Marxist theory as totalizing and reductive, claiming that it is blind to patriarchy and racism and that it denies cultural diversity. Instead, post-Marxists attend to difference, discourse, and identity, and talk not about revolution but about democracy (Dyer-Witheford 1999, 13). Partly this can be seen as a continuation of postmodern politics. Instead of arguing against capitalism and offering a vision of solidarity, many started to stress difference and identity. This does not really challenge capitalism but instead often coexists rather easily with it, for example in the form of fashion (Dean 2009, 34). Similarly, the postmodern emphasis on fluid and highly individual identities was highly compatible with neoliberal ideology. But partly it is more than that: there is an awareness of historical forms of injustice and some of the Marxian rhetoric of struggle, resistance, and systemic change has been taken up again, albeit without the focus on class and socio-economic categories, and with a rejection of universalism.

With regard to bias in AI and discrimination by AI, the relevant normative question is then: against what specific groups do these technologies and those who employ them discriminate, and which struggles for recognition are threatened by AI? Is there a bias against women? Against transgender people? Against black people? Against disabled people? A famous argument in the area of AI and robotics that draws on race is by Benjamin (2019a; 2019b), who has argued that these technologies are not politically neutral but deepen racial discrimination, inequality, and injustice. Writing in the context of a history (and, unfortunately, often present) of racial discrimination in the US, she claims that injustice is done to a particular group, black people. From this perspective, what is wrong with the biased algorithms in question is that they are not neutral but systematically disadvantage black people, thus reproducing existing inequality and contributing to "interlocking forms of discrimination" (Benjamin 2019b), in particular racial bias. Rhee (2018, 105), meanwhile, has claimed that the appearance of many companion robots and smart dolls "normalizes whiteness." Such arguments thus defuse the instrumentalist view that technology is neutral and radically oppose narratives – often coming from the corporate world – about neutral technology and about the digital as a place where there is an "even playing field" and even "where inequalities are rectified" (Benjamin 2019b, 133). Here this is done by looking at the problems through the lens of race and identity, rather than from a detached, universalist standpoint.

Consider again the unjustified arrest case at the beginning of this book. According to Benjamin and others who take a similar identity perspective, what was wrong in this case (and others like it) was not that in general and in the abstract a "person" or "citizen" was unjustly arrested, but that a *black* man was arrested *because he was black*: this was racism. Or to put it in terms of a popular slogan used in the context of a decade of protests in the US against racially motivated violence: the focus of this identity-based argument is not on "all lives matter" but on "black lives matter." Instead of what they perceive as the lofty "white" perspective of classical liberal theory, thinkers such as Benjamin prefer to look at what is really happening on the ground through the lens of race. They point out that universalist thinking has not been effective in creating a just and egalitarian society and claim that it has only served specific groups (e.g., white people, men).

For example, instead of appealing to universalist principles, Benjamin (2019b) calls for imagining "alternatives to the *techno quo* – business as usual when it comes to technoscience" by means of "a liberatory imagination" that "builds on a black racial tradition" (12). Here the political imagination feeds on particular (group and identity) histories rather than appealing to abstract conceptions of justice or equality.

A crucial aspect of identity thinking is the reference to the historical background. For example, when it comes to racial identity, defenders of identity politics point to the historical horrors of slavery and colonialism. This can be done in at least two compatible ways. One is to argue that the *present* injustices done to, say, black people in the US are not only rooted in racism (as if that were just a kind of abstract system of beliefs) but are also the continuation of these concrete and shockingly wrong historical forms of oppression and racist practices, albeit in forms that are not formally recognized as slavery and colonialism. Repairing bias in AI, then, is a way to contribute to fighting racism and to the total – not partial – abolition of these forms of oppression, preventing its continuation in the future. Criticisms that focus on (neo-)colonialism also take this historical angle. For example, Couldry and Mejias (2019) speak of "data colonialism" to express how present inequalities are a continuation of historical forms of empire and exploitation, at least "to the extent to which we are exploited through use of the data we create" (107–8). People's data, labor, and, in the end, social relations (12) are appropriated by capitalism. Moreover, use of AI in one place (by the privileged) relies on labor and exploitation elsewhere, far away. For example, the training of machine learning can involve such a form of exploitation.

The historical angle also brings us to the theme of colonialism. Against the background of historical colonialism, one can look critically at current AI and other technical practices by referring to the danger (or reality?) of neo-colonialism. For example, there is the concern that the universal humans and individuals addressed by liberal theory in practice stand for people living in affluent Western societies and that the interests and identity of the Global South are thereby neglected. While this concern can also be framed within liberalism and Marxism, for example by referring to socio-economic inequalities and injustices or to oppression of workers and geopolitics within a capitalist context, it can also be put in terms of identity and colonialism. For example, an opinion piece speaks about "digital colonialism" as the imperialist exploitation of poorer countries by powerful Silicon Valley tech corporations (Kwet 2019). Similarly, it has been argued (Birhane 2020) that "the AI invasion of Africa echoes colonial era exploitation," with the neglect of local needs and interests and the perpetuation of historical bias in a way that disadvantages minority groups (e.g., those without documents who are excluded from a national biometric system) amounting to the "algorithmic colonization" of that continent. (Some of these problems can also be addressed in terms of technology transfer, which often perpetuates undemocratic practices in developing countries. This can be seen as a form of colonialism and injustice against specific groups, but it can also be framed in terms of human rights violations.)

Another and compatible way to bring in history is to use it to warn that the present injustices, which may well be less bad than the historical one, could lead to worse forms of oppression in the *future*, and that this has to be stopped before that point is reached. In this example, racism and current forms of oppression are seen as necessarily leading to societies that systematically oppress and exploit people with a particular racial background, in other words societies based on colonial and slavery thinking. This is why racism in and through AI needs to be stopped. Another example is gender: gender bias in AI is seen as the continuation of historical forms of oppression and patriarchy, *and* as a problem that could lead to new forms of oppression and patriarchy. For example, there can be bias in language and in specific language corpora on the internet (e.g., a bias that links a particular profession such as medical doctor with males), and if this bias feeds into artificial intelligence and data science tools for natural language processing (Caliskan, Bryson, and Narayanan 2017; Sun et al. 2019), then this perpetuates historical bias that is present in texts *and* potentially aggravates the bias in the future.

Yet the focus is often on the continuation of historical bias. For example, commenting on predictive policing, Crawford and Calo (2016) use the language of identity politics when they say in *Nature* that we need to investigate how "AI systems disproportionately affect groups that are already disadvantaged by factors such as race, gender and socio-economic background" (312). It is also often claimed that AI may reflect bias against women due to bias present in the teams of often predominantly male developers of the technology, who in turn inherited that bias from previous generations. Thus, the reference point is historical and present forms of discrimination against specific groups, which are characterized in terms of identity (race, gender, etc.) rather than, for example, socio-economic criteria alone. Individual cases of discrimination and oppression here and now are seen in the light of historical discrimination against specific groups, defined in terms of identity and seeking recognition of that identity and that history. The historical angle is shared with Marxism, but the focus has shifted from defending the interests of a particular socio-economic class and promoting the goal of universal emancipation (Marxism) to the present concerns, history, and future of particular groups defined by their identity.

Similar history-based arguments can also be made against using and understanding robots as "slaves." The argument *for* using robots as slaves is that it stops exploitation of humans. Arguing against giving rights to robots, Bryson (2010) has claimed that robots should be legally considered as slaves. One could then deal with legal issues using Roman law, according to which the owner of the slaves is responsible for damages, as Floridi (2017) has proposed. However, as I suggested in the previous chapter, something seems wrong with thinking about robots in terms of slaves. The identity politics perspective now provides an argument why this wrong, which can be used instead of, or in addition to, the Marxian objection. Seen against the historical background of slavery and discrimination against specific groups, one could object to seeing robots as slaves by arguing that it perpetuates a history of thinking in terms of masters and slaves and a history of marginalizing and excluding a specific group. While no humans are harmed when robots are used as slaves, the kind of discourse and thinking about social relations is then seen as fundamentally problematic. Thus, the objection against seeing robots as slaves can be supported by universalist liberal or Marxian thinking, for example arguments against hegemonic and capitalist social relations, or by identity arguments, which link the enslavement of robots to the historical, present, and perhaps future marginalization of specific groups (of humans). Today the robots are the slaves; but perhaps tomorrow this might be extended to another group? Moreover, one could extend the scope of this argument to animals: is our treatment of some non-human animals not a form of slavery? I will say more about the politics with regard to non-humans in chapter 6, but here it is interesting to note that all these criticisms share the view that neither ancient Greek or Roman thinking about slaves, nor later developments in the history of philosophy that suppose or support these kinds of social hierarchies, are good sources for the normative evaluation of technologies, since they continue a form of hegemonic and colonial thinking. It is therefore important to critically study the discourses of political exclusion and domination that may accompany the use and development of AI.

Identity thinking remains controversial, in political philosophy and elsewhere. Even in feminist theory, which is often sympathetic to identity thinking, there have been discussions about what that feminine identity means, for example whether it is an essential identity or one that must be understood in performative terms (Butler 1999). Contemporary feminists have called for a post-identity politics that goes beyond "a parochial politics of recognition" and a politics of suffering based on victim identity, and instead attends to "a wider politics of diversity" (McNay 2010, 513) and the creation of freedom-enabling forms of life (514). For example, McNay (2008) has argued against reducing politics to issues of identity. But as was to be expected, there has also been criticism from both liberals and Marxians. Marxians accuse proponents of identity politics of occupying themselves only with the superstructure (culture) without paying attention to the underlying economics, thus focusing on marginalized groups but neglecting general economic structures that produce inequality and remaining tied to capitalist logic. They prefer to use the category of "class" to analyze and challenge socioeconomic inequality under capitalism. And Fukuyama (2018a) warns that societies guided by identity render deliberation and collective action difficult since they fracture into segments of identity. He also notes that the right uses the same language, for example to victimize white males, while the left breaks up into "a series of identity groups" (Fukuyama 2018b, 167). He proposes that in such democracies we need to "work our way back to more universal understandings of human dignity" (xvi).

For thinking about bias and AI, such discussions and their political context (e.g., the Black Lives Matter movement) remain relevant. How to frame bias and discrimination matters a lot, not only philosophically but also in practice. Should we build universalist principles of justice into our algorithms, or instead focus on bias against specific groups and take measures of positive discrimination, via the technology and in other ways? Should we accept historical bias present in language corpora (e.g., claim that the data imported from the internet mirror society as it is, that data and algorithms should be "neutral") or insist that algorithms are never neutral, that they are biased, and fix this bias, effectively contributing to a society that is less biased against historically disadvantaged groups? Could both types of arguments be combined, or are they incommensurable? Could aspects of both normative theories be implemented in practice? If so, what potential tensions might arise?

Conclusion: AI is not politically neutral

From the philosophy of technology, we know that technologies are not, and cannot be, morally and politically neutral. This is so in general (for all technologies) and it is also the case with AI and data science. While some people think that, as Matzner (2019, 109) puts it, "algorithms could be neutral, if humans would not constantly spoil them with their biases," this view is mistaken. Instead, the relation between humans and machines is far more complex, and this is also true for humans and AI. AI algorithms are never neutral, and both the bias in society and the biases that result from the algorithms and the data science processes need to be evaluated. Similarly, as Gitelman and Jackson (2013) have argued, data themselves are also not neutral, objective, or "raw." Instead, they are "produced by the operations of knowledge production" (3), involving interpretation, curation, and perception – including feelings (Kennedy, Steedman, and Jones 2020). As already mentioned, there can, for example, be bias in language corpora that are used by AI. Bias is also embedded in language itself, for example gender bias. Consider use of the English word "man" in a way that is supposed to refer not only to males but also to the human species in general (Criado Perez 2019, 4). In addition, as I have already suggested, teams dealing with data are also not neutral. People may be biased and teams may lack diversity of ethnicity and political opinion, for example when they mainly consist of white men, who share specific political opinions, including opinions about identity politics (Criado Perez 2019, 23). Technocracy is also not neutral or apolitical. Technical expertise alone cannot settle ethical and political debates. And tech companies have their own politics. For example, according to Murray (2019, 110), Silicon Valley companies such as Google are politically left (more accurately: left-libertarian) and expect this from their employees – even if what they preach is not always practiced, for example when it comes to the diversity of their own workforce. And tech companies such as Amazon or Uber also monitor the performance of their employees by means of AI and algorithms: Amazon uses AI to automatically fire low-productivity workers (Tangerman 2019) and Uber's algorithms rank its drivers, which governs how much they get paid and even if they get fired (Bernal 2020). Such practices, insofar as they are exploitative, contrast with their political discourse, and are themselves all but ethically or politically neutral. Finally, as I already noted in the previous chapter, beyond the immediate environment of the tech companies and their market, AI services rely on human labor in the Global South. The latter do not reap the fair rewards of their labor.

Given this non-neutrality of AI, data, and the people and organizations who deal with the technology, these technological operations, practices, interpretations, and perceptions need to be evaluated. However, that still leaves open the question of *how*, that is, on which basis this normative evaluation can be done. Therefore, it is of vital importance that we discuss the norms and the relevant concepts. In this chapter, this means that we discuss what we mean by bias and discrimination, (in)justice, (in)equality, and so on, and why exactly they are problematic. I have introduced another part of a normative, *political-philosophical* conceptual framework for evaluating AI: one based on notions such as equality and justice. This may inform discussions about the politics of AI also in those places where the technology is developed and used.

This additionally raises the question of *who* has to evaluate and do something about the problems. Developers of the technology have an important role here, since they are also responsible for the effects of their technologies. And partly they already take up this role: as employees who are stimulated to do so by the companies and organizations for whom they work, which at least pay lip service to the development of responsible AI; as entrepreneurs interested in more than making money; or as citizens who are themselves motivated to change things, for example as hackers. As Webb (2020) shows, in response to the digital revolution and the mass surveillance, concentration of power, and authoritarianisms that it enables, a struggle is taking place to disrupt and change things. Hacking is, then, part of a social movement and a new kind of activism that takes things into its own hands. As citizens, hackers fight "to take back their democracies" (4), perhaps also to preserve freedom and to achieve more justice and equality. Beyond that, one could also aim for broader citizen education on the political impact of AI. This then raises the problem of how to measure that impact, which is often difficult to predict (Djeffal 2019, 271). Moreover, the political significance and impact themselves may be contested. More and new tools need to be developed for exploring future and potential social and political significance and consequences of AI and for creating the conditions for a high-quality discussion about these possibilities. This is helpful both for developers of AI and for citizens.

More generally, given the vast and challenging discussions about fundamental political issues that loom in the background, tech workers, companies, organizations, governments, hackers, teachers, and citizens should not be left alone to responding to the politics of the AI challenge, and there should be a broader and public discussion about the topic. In democratic societies, we (citizens) should decide about the political direction. Together with the assistance of experts, this can help those who develop the technology create the lenses through which they can analyze bias in AI and, if needed, correct it in and through the technologies. Conceptual tools from political philosophy – in this chapter, discussions about justice and equality – can contribute to improving the quality of these democratic discussions, finding a normative direction, and redesigning the technologies. The next chapter further discusses the relation between AI and democracy.

4

Democracy: Echo Chambers and Machine Totalitarianism

Introduction: AI as a threat to democracy

Together with human rights and the rule of law, democracy is usually seen as one of the core elements of Western liberal constitutions (Nemitz 2018, 3) and liberal political thought. Many political systems in the world appeal to the ideal of democracy. Could AI strengthen democracy, or does it rather weaken it? What is the impact of AI on democracy, given its pervasive social and political consequences?

Today many critics warn that AI threatens democracy. Instead of helping to establish "a new Athenian Age of democracy;" as then Vice President Al Gore said about computer networking in a speech in the mid-1990s (Saco 2002, xiii), ushering in an age in which the internet and the use of AI create a new kind of political *agora*, it is feared that AI technologies lead to a less democratic world, if not a dystopia. Critics question the idea that technology is politically neutral or doubt that digital technologies such as the internet and AI necessarily lead to progress. For example, in *The Age of Surveillance Capitalism* (2019), Zuboff argues that surveillance capitalism, which uses mass behavior modification techniques, is a threat not only to individual autonomy but also to democracy, since it overthrows people's sovereignty. To argue why it is anti-democratic, she refers to Paine's *The Rights of Man*, which warns against aristocracy since such a body of people hold themselves accountable to nobody (513). This time, however, the tyranny does not come from aristocrats but from surveillance capitalism, a form of raw capitalism (518) that expropriates human experience and imposes a new kind of control: a concentration of knowledge means a concentration of power. Webb agrees in *The Big Nine* (2019): we are not in control since the big corporations shape our future. This is not democratic. Or as Diamond (2019) puts it: what is good for big tech is "not necessarily good for democracy – or even for our individual mental and physical health" (21). Moreover, not only citizens but also states become increasingly dependent on corporations and what they know about citizens (Couldry and Mejias, 2019, 13). Yet Zuboff (2019) still believes that reform is possible through democracy. Inspired by Hannah Arendt, she thinks that new beginnings are possible, that we can "reclaim the digital future as humanity's home" (525). By contrast, Harari argues in *Homo Deus* (2015) that in the future democracy might decline and disappear altogether since it cannot cope with the data: "As both the volume and speed of data increase, venerable institutions like elections, parties and parliaments might become obsolete" (373). Technological change is fast and politics can no longer catch up. Already now, crucial choices affecting our lives, for example choices concerning the internet, have not been through democratic processes. Even dictators are overwhelmed by the pace of technological change.

This chapter further investigates the impact of AI on democracy by visiting political-philosophical theory about democracy and its conditions, including the relation between knowledge/ expertise and democracy, and by inquiring about the origins of totalitarianism. First, it outlines the tension between, on the one hand, Platonic and technocratic conceptions of politics that emphasize knowledge, education, and expertise of the rulers and, on the other hand, ideals of participative and deliberative democracy à la Dewey and Habermas, which in turn have been criticized by Mouffe and Rancière, who offer a different, radical and agonistic ideal of democracy and politics. It asks how AI may threaten or support these different ideals and conceptions of democracy. For example, AI could be used for enabling direct democracy, but it might also support authoritarian technocracy: a rule by experts or – as Harari suggests – by AI itself. And if democracy requires that citizens have information about each other's views and engage in deliberation geared towards consensus, then digital technology could facilitate that, but there are also some phenomena that lead to fragmentation and polarization of the public sphere and thus threaten this ideal of democracy. Finally, AI may be used by those who seek to destroy the political itself: as a tool for Platonic philosopher-kings or Habermasian democracy, it could be used to push a rationalist and technosolutionist understanding of politics, which ignores the inherently agonistic dimension of politics and risks excluding other points of view.

Second, the chapter asks if AI may contribute to creating the conditions for totalitarianism. Based on Arendt's (2017) work on the origins of totalitarianism, it considers whether AI supports a society in which loneliness and lack of trust create a fertile soil for totalitarian tendencies. And if AI is used as a tool for the corporate and bureaucratic management of people via data, then this treats people as things and can – through the often-unintended consequences of people who *just do their job* – lead to what Arendt (2006) called "the banality of evil." This not only is a problem of the historical past but also constitutes a present danger, when our data are in the hands of people in tech companies and government administrations who may do what their managers and politicians tell them to do and stop *thinking*.

AI as a threat to democracy, knowledge, deliberation, and politics itself

Starting with Plato: Democracy, knowledge, and expertise

To know if and how AI may threaten democracy, we first have to know what democracy is. Let us look at different views of democracy and its conditions, including the relation between knowledge/expertise and democracy.

Democracy is an answer to the ancient question: who should rule? Democracy theory often responds to Plato, who rejected democracy and argued that to rule necessitates knowledge, in particular knowledge of the good and justice. In the *Republic*, he associates democracy with ignorance and argues that it leads to tyranny. Using the analogy of navigation, he proposes that a good leader should be knowledgeable since, as captain, he needs to be able to control the ship of the state. Another analogy Plato uses is that of a medical doctor: if you are ill, you want expert advice. Ruling the state is a matter of craft and expertise. Therefore, philosophers should rule, since they are in love with wisdom and the search for reality and truth. With "philosophy," Plato did not mean academic philosophy: in the *Republic*, he makes clear that his guardians would also receive musical, mathematical, military, and physical training (Wolff 2016, 68). Giving power to the people, by contrast, would mean letting ignorance, hysteria, pleasure, and cowardice rule. Without appropriate leadership, political conflict and ignorance would result in demands for a strong leader, a tyrant.

This view changes in modern times when new conceptions of human nature and politics arise according to which the many, not just the few, are capable of self-rule. For example, Rousseau's thinking also aims to steer away from tyranny, but for him the solution to the Platonic problem of authority is not the rule of the educated few, but the education of all citizens: self-rule is possible and desirable, provided all citizens receive moral education (Rousseau 1997). Rousseau thus stood at the basis of another strand in political theory, which believes in democracy and broadens self-rule to all citizens *and* adds some conditions to self-rule. But which conditions should this self-rule adopt, and which form should it take? It is one thing to say that democracy should not be a matter of rule by philosopher-kings; it is quite another to specify what knowledge is necessary for democracy, if any, and to define the precise form democracy should take. For example, should democracy involve deliberation and participation? And how can and does AI relate to this form of democracy?

Let's start with the question regarding knowledge and democracy. One discussion in political theory that is pertinent to our discussion is the technocracy/democracy debate, which began with Plato, if not earlier, and which acquired a new relevance with the rise of modern bureaucracies. During recent decades, there have been calls for data-driven decisions, smart governance, and scientific, evidence-based policies, which are in tension with calls for participatory governance and more radical forms of democracy. The divergences between these different arguments and languages (Gilley 2016) reflect opposing views on the role of knowledge and expertise in politics.

Often AI is perceived as being firmly on the side of technocracy. It offers new possibilities to generate knowledge about social reality – one could also say: to construct social reality. The science of statistics had already long been used in modern governance, but with machine learning the possibilities of predictive analysis expand. Couldry and Mejiaas (2019) talk about a new social epistemology that is enabled by AI. AI creates new power for the technocratic steering of society, which contrasts with democratic ideals. AI seems to be a domain for experts, beyond most people's understanding. For example, Pasquale (2019, 1920) has argued that for a fair distribution of expertise and power, incentives need to be created for individuals to understand AI and its supply chain. If this does not happen, we may well become totally dependent on AI and the bureaucrats who use it to control us. Transhumanists such as Harari even think that AI will rule us in the future. But leaving science fiction aside, it could be argued that we are already ruled by big corporations who use AI to manipulate us – totally outside democratic control, as Zuboff pointed out. Who should rule is a merely theoretical question when we are already ruled by Google, Amazon, and other large corporate players. In that sense, there is something essentially anti-democratic about AI. Moreover, is the kind of knowledge AI offers sufficient for decision-making? It could be argued that there is a gap that requires human judgment and democratic deliberation. The kind of intelligence AI displays is also often contrasted with human social intelligence, which seems needed for political discourse and social meaning-making in democracies. But could AI also support more democratic forms of government and governing, and if so, how? To develop this discussion, we need to further investigate the central question of what democracy is and what it requires in terms of knowledge.

Beyond majority rule and representation

Many people mean by democracy the rule of the majority and think of a representative form of democracy. But both views of democracy can and have been contested. For a start, it is not clear that *democracy as majority rule* is necessarily a good thing. As Dworkin (2011) puts it: "Why should the fact that numerically more people favour one course of action over another signal that the more favoured policy is either fairer or better?"

Consider, for example, that, under the sway of a demagogic leader, a majority may decide to abolish democracy and install an authoritarian government – something Plato already warned against. At the very least, democracy as majority rule does not seem a sufficient condition for democracy: perhaps it is necessary, but more is needed. Some would add the need for freedom or equality: values that are often cemented into liberal-democratic constitutions. Others would add some more Platonic elements, such as the requirement that political decisions be good (since majority rule does not guarantee a good outcome), which of course raises the question of what a good decision and outcome is, or the requirement that rulers need to have certain skills and knowledge. Should they be morally good, as Plato and Rousseau argued? In any case, one could argue that even in a democracy, some qualities of leadership are necessary. Bell (2016) claims that political merit is determined through three attributes: the political leader's intellectual ability, his or her social skills (including emotional intelligence – see Chou, Moffitt, and Bryant 2020), and his or her virtue. The latter is in line with Plato. Against the Platonic view, Estlund (2008) has argued that the Platonic conception of political authority as expertise confuses experts with bosses. He calls it the expert/boss fallacy: some people have more expertise than others, but "it simply does not follow from their expertise that they have authority over us, or that they ought to" (3). But if we separate the question of political authority from the question regarding expertise, does that mean that expertise and personal qualities should play no role at all in a democracy? Is bureaucratic steering totally unavoidable in the context of nation states as we know them? And is the use of AI for influencing behavior also permissible or even desirable under some conditions, or does this necessarily lead to authoritarianism? A rejection of technocracy leaves open the question of what role exactly experts, expertise, and technology should play in a democracy.

Moreover, *representative democracy* as we know it has also been contested: some think that only direct democracy is real democracy. Yet this seems hard to realize in the context of (large) nation states. The ancient version of democracy took place in the city state, and Rousseau had the city state he knew in mind (Geneva). Would this be a better level for governance, or is direct democracy possible even in the modern nation state? Could AI help with this, and if so, how precisely?

There are alternatives to representative democracy and majority rule, which at the same time avoid the Platonic views of political authority: *participative* and *deliberative*, consensus-directed ideals of democracy. Sometimes these conceptions of democracy are formulated as an answer to populism, which is accused of disregarding valuable norms of public debate "like telling the truth, engaging with others' reasons and respecting the evidence" (Swift 2019, 96). This assumes that further conditions need to be added to democracy as majority rule and representation; the idea is that democracy requires more from citizens than simply voting once in a while or having the majority rule. One meaning of democracy, for example, is democracy as public justification and deliberation: free and reasoned debate among equals is meant to lead to reasoned consensus among citizens (Christiano and Bajaj 2021). Such a conception of democracy can be found for example in Habermas, Rawls, Cohen, and O'Neill, who believe in a link between democracy and the use of public reason and deliberation. For example, in line with Habermas, Goodin has argued in *Reflective Democracy* (2003) for a form of democratic deliberation in which people imagine themselves in the position of others. Instead of limiting democracy to people's "external" act of voting, he proposes to focus on the "internal" acts and processes that should underlie it, in particular their reflective and considered judgments and joint determination of what collectively ought to be done (1). With "reflective," he means, among other things, that people are "more empathetic with the plight of others," also with those distant and with different interests, through imagining themselves in the place of the other (7). Facts and beliefs are also important, not just (conflicting) values (16).

Thus, we may distinguish between a "thin" or processual, formal ideal of democracy, which is about giving people a say through voting, and "thick" ideals that include some conditions such as deliberation, knowledge/expertise, and imagination, which renders democracy richer than the "mere aggregation of people's votes" (Goodin 2003, 17). However, from an Enlightenment perspective and in order to avoid an elite or Platonic-authoritarian version of democracy and support participatory forms of democracy, it is important to involve and educate all citizens. But increasing participation is challenging.

For example, giving people a direct vote does not necessarily increase their participation in politics (Tolbert, McNeal, and Smith 2003), and there are many forms of political activities available to the public, including political engagement online, for example via social media. In any case, participatory democracy takes seriously people's own potential to make political decisions, rather than delegating this to a philosopher-king or elite group. Participatory ideals of democracy oppose Platonic pessimism about rule by "mobs" and, influenced by Rousseau and other Enlightenment thinkers, have more trust in ordinary citizens and their capacities for deliberation and political participation.

What does this mean for AI? This kind of democracy rules out non-participatory forms of governance, such as *exclusive* and technocratic governance by experts and AI, and *blind* and exclusive reliance on algorithms and recommendations by AI. However, it leaves open the possibility that experts and knowledge gained with the help of AI can be somehow involved in the democratic process, as long as citizens themselves have the last word and can rely on their judgment and discussion. Yet the precise form any potential involvement of AI could take is not clear. In practice, AI and data science are already involved in democratic decision-making, but since most existing types of democracy are not highly deliberative and participative, it is hard to say how this combination could work. And there remains a tension between human judgment and machine calculation and prediction.

Let us take a closer look at deliberative and participatory democracy theory, but also its radical critics.

Deliberative and participatory democracy versus agonistic and radical democracy

In *deliberative* democracies, citizens apply practical intelligence in public deliberation between equals in which they do not only care about their own aims and interests, but also respond to those of others (Estlund 2008). Here democracy is about free public reasoning and discussion, and creating the conditions for this discussion (Christiano 2003). Habermas sees this as a process of rational political communication: communication guided by reason. His account famously relies on the "ideal speech situation," in which the course of deliberation is guided only by the power of reason, free of non-rational coercive influences and motivated by the desire for consensus. Later, presuppositions of argumentation formed the basis for his discourse ethics (Habermas 1990). According to Estlund (2008), this approach introduces values that go beyond democracy itself, since it transcends a procedural understanding of democracy. But deliberative democracy's proponents might reply that democracy cannot be reduced to a voting procedure and needs to involve the public use of reason. Argumentation and deliberation is, then, not an "extra" that is added on to the ideal of democracy – say, another value or principle – but an essential part of the concept. Moreover, taking into account Goodin and (other) further developments in Habermasian thinking, one could also add perspective-taking and solidarity. One could also reconnect "practical intelligence" to the ancient term *phronesis*: citizens would then need to develop practical wisdom, including – as we can add with Arendt – their political imagination.

There are also other theories of democracy that go beyond democracy as voting or representation, and emphasize the importance of communication. For example, Dewey's ideal of *participative* democracy requires active participation of citizens and stresses again the knowledge requirement: people need education in order to participate in politics. In *Democracy and Education* (2001), he argues for an ideal of democracy that is not just a form of government but a specific kind of society: "A democracy is more than a form of government; it is primarily a mode of associated living, of conjoint communicated experience" (91). More generally, the point of politics is to build the social. However, for Dewey, proximity or working towards a common end is not enough for a relationship to become really social. He reflects on the machine analogy: parts of a machine work together to reach a common result, but that is not a social group or a community. It is still too mechanical. For real sociality and community, communication is essential. If we want to work towards a common end and find consensus, we need communication: "[E]ach would have to know what the other was about and would have to have some way of keeping the other informed as to his own purpose and progress" (9). Moreover, participation requires education, "which gives individuals a personal interest in social relationships and control, and the habits of mind which secure social changes without introducing disorder" (104).

Dewey admits that this ideal of democracy sounds Platonic, but rejects the latter's class authoritarianism. He says Plato's ideal was "compromised in its working out by making a class rather than an individual the social unit" (104) and that it had no place for change. He also rejects 19th-century nationalism. Dewey has a more inclusive conception of democracy; it is supposed to be a way of living and a communicative experience for all individuals, not just for a particular class. He believes that individuals can be educated to develop acceptable modes of behavior. Thus, for Dewey, democracy is about individuals as interconnected, communicative beings. It is made by means of interaction and communication. It requires work: while we are born as social beings in the sense that we are associated with others, community and democracy need to be made. And they are made by all citizens, not just by a limited number of representatives.

However, the idea that democracy should be deliberative and aimed at consensus has received criticism from radical thinkers such as Young, Mouffe, and Rancière. In her book *Inclusion and Democracy* (2000), Young criticizes especially the Habermasian conception: for her, politics is not just about argument or dispassionate expression, and democracy should be more *inclusive* and communicative in the sense of also incorporating new voices and other styles and ways of speaking. Deliberation based on the best argument ignores styles of speech and presentation that are subordinated to the ways educated people express themselves. Norms of dialogue may exclude. People can also express themselves in a different way, for example through the public telling of stories (Young 2000; see also Martínez-Bascuñán 2016). Young (2000) defends a conception of political inclusion that transcends voting and emphasizes communication: "The normative legitimacy of a democratic decision depends on the degree to which those affected by it have been included in the decision-making processes" (6). This requires more than voting rights: Young argues that we need to consider modes of communication, representation, and organizing, and we should not restrict our conception of political communication to argument. In deliberative democracies, particular styles of expression are preferred, and this excludes other styles and specific people. While there has been an effort to interpret Habermas (and Kant) in a way that makes room for emotions and rhetoric (Thorseth

2008), Young thus recognizes the role of emotions and other styles of doing politics.

Mouffe replies to Habermas and other deliberative and consensus-directed ideals of democracy by stressing political confrontation and difference: difference will, and should, always remain, and there is no hope for redemption from strife. Against Platonic and rationalist ideals of politics and democracy, she thinks that there is no lasting political solution for all conflicts. Instead, conflict is a sign that democracies are alive. This is what she calls the *agonistic* dimension of politics. She understands the political as "the antagonistic dimension which is inherent in all human societies" (Mouffe 2016; see also Mouffe 1993; 2000; 2005): it can never be eliminated, regardless of the specific political practices and institutions. This also means that exclusion is unavoidable. A rational consensus without exclusion, an "us" without a "them," is not possible. Conflict in democratic societies should not be eradicated. Political identities are created in a way that demarcates an "us" from a "them" (see also chapter 6). Moreover, like Young, Mouffe recognizes the role of emotions alongside reason: the "passions" also play a role. However, conflict does not mean war: others should be seen not as enemies but as adversaries, opponents. This understanding of democracy recognizes the reality of strife in social life (Mouffe 2016). There are not rational or objective ways of organizing society; such solutions are also the result of power relations. Rational consensus is a fantasy. Instead, Mouffe proposes agonistic pluralism: a system based on constructive disagreement. As Farkas (2020) notes, Mouffe is influenced by Wittgenstein, who thought that any agreement in opinions must rely on agreement in forms of life. A fusion of voices is possible not as a product of reason but by a common form of life (Mouffe 2000, 70). Against Habermas and deliberative and rationalist approaches in general, Mouffe argues for fostering "a plurality of forms of being a democratic citizen" (73). If we fail to establish this agonistic pluralism, the alternative is authoritarianism, in which the leaders are supposed to take objective and true decisions.

Rancière also argues against Platonic and consensus-direct ideals of democracy, and rejects both management by specialists and representative democracy. Influenced by a particular version of socialism, he argues that to reject direct democracy is to have an attitude of condescension towards classes of people who lack education. Instead, he proposes to hear what the workers have to say. His version of politics and democracy favors political action rooted in disagreement and dissensus. In *Disagreement* (1999) and *Dissensus* (2010), he argues that demonstrations of equality occur when inequalities embedded in the current order are interrupted and reconfigured. And this is needed. Rancière questions whether representation and democracy belong together. He thinks that our institutions are representative but not democratic; they are oligarchic. But "there is no good reason as to why some men should rule others" (Rancière 2010, 53). The power of the ruling classes should be contested. Democracy should not be blamed for the instability of the representative system. He criticizes the distinction between the ignorant mass and the lucid, reasonable elite. Not even a crisis justifies the rule of experts and specialists. In an interview (Confavreux and Rancière 2020) he says: "Our governments have been operating for some time now under the alibi of an impending crisis that prevents the world's affairs from being entrusted to its ordinary inhabitants and requires that they be left to the care of crisis management specialists." Instead, he thinks that ordinary people are perfectly capable of acquiring knowledge. In *The Ignorant Schoolmaster* (1991), he suggests that "all men have equal intelligence" (18), that the poor and disenfranchised can teach themselves, and that we should not be bound to experts for our intellectual emancipation.

Influenced by Mouffe and Rancière, Farkas and Schou (2020) have intervened in the fake news and post-truth debate by arguing against equating the idea of democracy with "the ideas of reason, rationality and truth in an *a priori* fashion" (5). They question the view that what is threatening democracies is simply falsehood. Against Habermas and in line with Mouffe and Rancière, they see democracy as continuously evolving and as remaining the object of political and social struggle. They also question representative democracy: democracy is not just about voting, and reason cannot save democracy. They argue against truth-based solutionism, a single formula for the political community, the ideal of a rational consensus, and basing consensus on truth and reason. Rather, democracy has always produced different truths (rather than *the* Truth with a capital "T") and there are multiple grounds or foundations; if about truth at all, democracy is about that difference, plurality, and multiplicity:

> What remains proper to a well-functioning democracy is not so much its ability to navigate based on reason and truth, but its ability to include and give voice to different political projects and groups. Democracy is about different visions of how society should be organized. It is about affect, emotions, and feelings. (Farkas and Schou 2020, 7)

Farkas (2020) warns that "fake news" can become a rhetorical weapon to attack one's opponents and asks: who gets to draw the line between fake and real? Who gets to establish themselves as authorities? And if the meaning of politics, truth, and post-truth is performed and constructed, one should ask: who performs which truth discourses and why? In line with Derrida, Farkas and Schou (2018) believe that closure of meaning relies on exclusion and that discourses are always the result of "particular fixations of meaning resulting from political struggles that have repressed alternative pathways over time" (301). This approach does not mean that expertise no longer has any place in a democracy; rather, such tensions remain a dynamic in liberal democracies and democracy has to balance those forces. Moreover, new technologies such as AI can help to realize this ideal of democracy. Farkas and Schou (2020, 9) believe that pairing digital technologies to more participatory and inclusionary forms of democracy is the only way forward.

I will revisit the issue of emotions in the next chapter. For now, it is clear that there is a tension between those (from Plato to Habermas) who appeal to expertise, truth, reason, and consensus, on the one hand, and those who see democracy as struggle and/or direct participation, on the other: the rule of the people instead of the rule of reason, as Farkas and Schou (2020, 7) put it. Both deliberative-participative and agonistic ideals of democracy go against warnings that ordinary people may favor authoritarianism or are apathetic (see, e.g., Dahl 1956 or Sartori 1987 – as Sartori put it: voters seldom act, they "react" [123]) and against the view, for example defended by Schumpeter, that "ordinary people are simply not *competent* to understand the issues that lie behind political decisions, and so they are happy to hand these decisions over to people they regard as better qualified to deal with them" (Miller 2003, 40; Miller's emphasis).

But how can people acquire the competence? Is self-education sufficient, as Rancière thinks, or do we need general education, as Dewey proposes? Dewey's ideal of democracy is non-representative. But even in a representative system, one could argue that people need education in order to be able to better choose their representatives. Moreover, education counters the danger of authoritarianism. The point would not be to give more votes to the better educated, as Mill proposed and which accords with the Platonic view, but rather to educate everyone.

Can science and technology help to overcome ignorance with such an education? Much depends on how science and technology is used, and what kind of knowledge is offered. Facts are required but may not change the minds of people, and as we will see below, information alone is not enough. Furthermore, there is the danger of replacing politics with science, technology, and good management. Political use of AI is often mobilized or supported by those who think that the struggles and the messy complexity of politics can be reduced to rational decision-making and finding outcomes that are objectively better than others. There is the Platonic temptation of turning politics into a question about philosophical truth and expertise. In "Two Concepts of Liberty" (see chapter 2), Berlin already warned against turning all political problems into technological ones: if everyone agrees on the ends, then the only questions left concern the means: they can be "settled by experts or machines" and government becomes what Saint-Simon called "the administration of things" (Berlin 1997, 191). Moreover, scientific knowledge may well be necessary for political judgment, but it is certainly not sufficient. Magnani (2013) has argued that the knowledge we need in morality should not only be scientific "but also human and social, embedded in reshaped 'cultural' traditions," and we need a morality "capable of dealing with the new global condition of human life" by taking into account that consequences are often spatially or temporality distant (68); the latter requires imagination. The same could be said about political knowledge. Furthermore, one could argue that making politics more inclusive and less technocratic and relying on pooled and collective intelligence, as Dewey proposed, is one way to deal with these problems, since it brings in social and situated knowledge: knowledge embedded in, and shaped by, concrete historical and cultural contexts, which science does not (easily?) provide. This may help the political imagination.

But if democracy needs to be more deliberative and partici- pative, what is the role of AI then? Can it help the kind of deliberation, communication, participation, and imagination envisaged by the theorists discussed here? Or is it a mere tool for manipulating voters and, more generally, for turning people into things (data)? Can it help public reasoning, or is it a threat to such an ideal, given that it may not be transparent that it makes recommendations and how it makes recommendations, and that – in the form of machine learning at least – the way it works has nothing to do with reasoning or judgment? And can people (including politicians) have sufficient knowledge and skills to deal with the information offered by AI and data science, or are we in the hands of a technocratic elite who know what is good for us? What if AI offers, to use Scanlon's phrase, a rule which "no one could reasonably reject" (Scanlon 1998, 153)? Does AI mainly create an environment for Platonic modes of governance, or is a democracy à la Habermas or Dewey possible? Will AI be used on the side of reason and objectivity, potentially against the people, who are deemed too emotional? Could it also play a role in agonistic and radical democracy, including maintaining difference and fostering the emancipation of all? One way to further discuss these questions is to point to the problem of information bubbles and echo chambers, to which we now turn.

Information bubbles, echo chambers, and populism

Based on these ideals of deliberative and agonistic democracy, one could propose that smart technologies such as AI should contribute to enabling broad, inclusive political participation via social media. But then we should consider the challenges and limitations of these technologies in terms of knowledge.

Some of these issues with the internet and social media were already known in media studies. For example, Sunstein (2001) analyzed problems related to personalization, fragmentation, and polarization, and Pariser (2011) argued that personalization creates a filter bubble that limits our horizon. But now the combination of social media and AI exacerbates these tendencies. The issue has been formulated in terms of information bubbles and echo chambers (see, e.g., Niyazov 2019): personalization algorithms feed people with information with which they are likely to engage and the result is segregation into bubbles where their own beliefs are reinforced and they are not exposed to opposite views. This renders the political imagination Goodin (2003) envisages more difficult: it seems to hinder rather than promote empathic forms of politics. There is also more political polarization, which renders both consensus and collective action impossible; there is a risk of fragmentation and the breakdown of society. Social media are seen as especially problematic: while print publications, TV, and radio have echo chambers of their own, they still "exercise some degree of editorial control" (Diamond 2019, 22). This is lacking in social media echo chambers, which leads to polarization and hateful language.

This is problematic if one wants to have a rational, consensus-oriented debate *à la* Habermas. But even an agonistic form of democracy is difficult when people are not exposed to opposite views. El-Bermawy (2016) has argued that the global village has been replaced by "digital islands of isolation that are drifting further apart each day." There is more segregation. On Facebook, we mostly consume political content similar to our views. In this way, we develop tunnel vision. Nguyen (2020) distinguishes between epistemic bubbles, which leave out relevant voices (often not intentionally), and echo chambers, which are a structure from which other relevant voices have been actively excluded and in which people come to distrust all outside sources. Search engines, for instance, may trap users in filter bubbles and echo chambers through the way they function, threatening diversity and thereby democracy (Granka 2010). This is certainly a risk, although empirical work finds that social media also expose users to opposing perspectives and that only a small group of users deliberately seek out echo-chamber-style opinion environments (Puschmann 2018). Social media also enable people to publish opinions that would be censored out of major news outlets. In this sense, there is at least a chance of diversity of opinions.

However, according to deliberative ideals of democracy, democracy is not just about the exchange of opinions, and goes beyond temporary concerns. For example, the deliberative ideal of democracy is about the public use of reason and includes deliberating how to live together over a longer time and about commitments. Benhabib (interviewed in Wahl-Jorgensen 2008) argues against views that reduce democracy to "the unfettered exchange of opinion" via the internet and neglect long-term "action commitments" (965) such as giving part of your income to the community. AI may also threaten the communicative rationality and the public sphere envisaged by Habermas, Arendt, and others. According to Benhabib, it is a challenge "to conceptualize the interaction between these networks of communication, information and opinion building, on the one hand, and public articulation in terms of decisional articulation, on the other" (964).

Formulated in terms of knowledge, one could argue that echo chambers threaten the epistemic foundation of democracy – at least according to deliberative, participative, and republican accounts of democracy. As Kinkead and Douglas (2020) frame the problem: political thinkers from Rousseau and Mill to Habermas, Goodin, and Estlund believe in the epistemic power, virtue, and justification of democracy, since free public debate allows us to track the truth and share and discuss a diversity of views (121). However, social media combined with big data analytics change the nature of political communication: instead of exposing one's views to public discussion and scrutiny by broadcasting, it is now possible to send highly targeted messages to many people all over the world, to "narrowcast political messages with global reach" (129). This has epistemic consequences:

> One risk to the epistemic virtue of democracy is that closed social networks appropriate the public sphere and make it private. Once private and shared only among similar individuals, political discourse loses some of its epistemic robustness as ideas are no longer challenged by diverse perspectives. (127)

In addition, in private discourse, it is easier to use manipulation without this being noticed by the participants (127–8). Consider also again Mill's view that better ideas and truth will emerge in an open marketplace of ideas: this openness is threatened by echo chambers, filter bubbles, and narrowcasting.

More generally, one could argue that this privatization of the public sphere is highly problematic from a democratic point of view, since democracy requires a *public* sphere and politics is about public affairs; phenomena such as echo chambers endanger this. But what is the public sphere anyway, and what is "public" in the light of current digital technologies? The public/private distinction seems obsolete when people share their most private thoughts and feelings on social media, and technology and politics based on identity also put pressure on the distinction. Nevertheless, for the reasons offered by deliberative theories of democracy, it is good to retain and defend a notion of "public." Additionally, one could point to the need for collective solutions to collective problems. Couldry, Livingstone, and Markham (2007) write that just as citizenship is not simply a lifestyle choice, public issues and politics "involve more than just 'social belonging' or expressions of identity [see also again the arguments against identity politics]. Something crucial remains at stake in the public/private distinction, notwithstanding postmodernist thinkers who celebrate its breakdown" (6). They argue that democracy requires a notion of some issues that are public and that require a common definition and collective solution. But technology may not make it easy to distinguish between public and private concerns. And political criticism may often be excluded from the public sphere called "politics" and take place in other spheres such as art and indeed social media, which may or may not be public, or public only in some aspects.

A related issue is populism, which may link to AI in various ways. For example, populist politicians use AI to analyze data about voters' preferences. But while it is good in a democracy that politicians know what citizens need, this use of AI "could turn into demagogic mass appeals, rather than the reasoned deliberation process envisioned, for example, by the Founding Fathers of the United States" (Niyazov 2019). Some theorists are more positive about populism. According to Laclau (2005), populism is not just an ontic, empirical reality (a particular kind of politics) but is synonymous with politics; it is about the political as such. He sees the possibility of a renewed political project. But most theories considered here, and movements such as Occupy, distance themselves from populism. In any case, in social media we see the valorization and glorification of commentary from non-elites and a dismissal of expert knowledge (Moffitt 2016), which has been called "epistemological populism" (Saurette and Gunster 2011). Moffitt (2016) sees positive sides to this, for example uncovering of corruption, but also points to the echo chambers. Social media can contribute to the spread of populism and to more ideological division and the favoring of virality and immediacy over the politics of discussion and understanding. While social media are not necessarily AI driven, AI may play a role in this by filtering and regulating the information and in the form of bots, which influence political communication and potentially also voters' preferences. This may prepare society for an authoritarian leader who claims to embody the will of the people and whose personal obsessions become those of the nation. AI, through social media, can contribute to this rise of populism and, eventually, authoritarianism.

More problems: Manipulation, replacement, accountability, and power

AI can be used to manipulate people. I already mentioned the possibilities for nudging, which influences decisions (see chapter 2). Like other digital technologies, it can even be used to shape human experience and thought. As Lanier (2010) puts it, speaking in the name of technologists: "We tinker with your philosophy by direct manipulation of your cognitive experience, not indirectly, through argument. It takes only a tiny group of engineers to create technology that can shape the entire future of human experience with incredible speed" (7). In the context of representative democracy and its voting procedures, AI and other digital technologies can nudge voters towards supporting a particular politician or party through personalized advertisements, and so on. Niyazov (2019) argues that this may lead to the tyranny of the minority (the swing voters). A known case that concerned the manipulation of people is that of Cambridge Analytica (see chapter 2), which involved harvesting private data from Facebook users without their permission. It has been claimed that those data were then used for the purpose of influencing political processes, for example by Donald Trump's 2016 presidential campaign. Keeping in mind Bell's (2016) criteria for political leadership, the manipulative use of AI may also mirror a shift away from intelligence, social skills, and virtue. And if AI were to take over political leadership at all, it is doubtful that AI could ever have the intellectual capacities, social skills, and virtue required, according to Bell.

Replacement of human leadership by AI is in any case

dangerous and anti-democratic. The danger is not just that an AI that takes over may destroy humanity, but also that it rules, or claims to rule, *in the best interests of humanity*. This is a classic science-fiction trope (see, e.g., the film *I, Robot* or Neal Asher's *Polity* novels) and a danger according to all ideals of democracy: it destroys liberal democracy, since it destroys freedom as autonomy of citizens, and, in the end, it also robs us of politics as such, as Damnjanović (2015) has argued. This scenario could only be supported by a very particular interpretation of Plato in which AI would act as an artificial philosopher-king (perhaps combined with a modern utilitarian argument that aims for maximizing utility for humanity as a whole or a Hobbesian argument that aims for the survival and peace of humankind). The captain or steerman (*kybernetes*) of the ship of the state then becomes an autopilot. Perhaps it could even navigate humanity as a whole and the planet. Such visions are rightly criticized by all democracy theories we have considered here. It is also not clear if such an AI would command *de facto* authority, regardless of whether it is right and just to have such an AI authority.

From a philosophy of technology point of view, such scenarios and discussions show that AI is not just a technology but is always already linked to moral and political possibilities. They illustrate AI's non-instrumentality: AI is not just a tool for politics, but changes politics itself. Furthermore, even if AI is used within a democratic framework, there is a problem of accountability and legitimacy when decisions are based on AI's recommendations, especially if it is not transparent how these decisions were taken or if biases are introduced or reproduced during the process. A well-known example is AI that helps US judges in matters of criminal sentencing, parole, and eligibility for social services (see the COMPAS case mentioned in chapter 3). For a democracy, public accountability is crucial: public officials who take decisions about citizens should be held accountable, and it is not clear how this can be maintained if they rely on AI for their decisions to a high degree and if the way AI arrives at its decisions is neither transparent nor neutral. The latter is also important since, as mentioned at the end of chapter 2, one could see equality as a condition for democracy. From this perspective, it is also highly problematic if we are controlled by a monopolized tech industry, which controls data and its flows, and therefore ultimately the people. Nemitz (2018) has criticized today's digital power concentration. He argues that the challenges posed by AI cannot only be addressed by AI ethics, but need to be dealt with by enforceable and legitimate rules that are the outcome of a democratic process. He calls for an AI culture that is democratic.

The power of big tech also poses a problem when it comes to dealing with fake news and disinformation. While fake news – false or misleading information presented as news – is also mobilized in technodeterministic, overly pessimistic critiques of digital media technologies (Farkas and Schou 2018, 302), these phenomena pose a serious political problem also with regard to democracy. What counts as "fake news," and who decides this? Should social media companies such as Twitter and Facebook become the censors, those who decide what content is allowed and what not, rather than, say, a democratically elected body? And if so, how should they deal with this? As noted, internet companies use content moderation – read: censorship. Given the size of current social media platforms and the short time windows, this partial or full automation of content moderation seems unavoidable. But it means that the rules of public speech (and the rules for what counts as facts and truth!) are set by a small group of Silicon Valley elites. It amounts to a hidden kind of governance, away from the spotlight of democratic institutions. Again, there is lack of transparency and accountability. It is also not clear how complex issues concerning justice can be dealt with; there is even a risk that they are depoliticized (Gorwa, Binns, and Katzenbach 2020). Furthermore, algorithms may let hate speech flourish, but they may also restrict the freedom of users to access content and express their opinion. It is not clear if the rights of users are sufficiently protected. And speech regulation by algorithms does not necessarily reflect societal trade-offs. Checks and balances are missing to ensure that power is exercised in the interests of society at large (Elkin-Koren 2020). AI's capacities are limited when it comes to dealing effectively with this issue – and all other complex political issues. Moreover, from a Marxian perspective, one could say that free speech itself becomes a commodity, something that is transformed into economic value in the data economy. What do political freedom and political participation mean in this context? And who defines the terms on which public discussion is conducted? A small number of powerful actors set the terms and conditions. So-called user "agreements," by which users agree to the terms set by platforms like Facebook or Twitter, are not democratic constitutions but dictates. This issue highlights again that AI does not just function as a politically neutral tool in the hands of humans playing a particular political game, but transforms the game itself, transforms the conditions under which politics is done. AI mediates and shapes democracy itself. Niyazov (2019) believes that open societies can deal with challenges regarding democracy and equality since they provide avenues for critical thinking. But what if open societies get transformed into something else, something much more opaque and hostile to critical thinking?

Note also that in democracies, difficult trade-offs need to be made between different political values, for example freedom and equality. As we saw in chapter 2, Tocqueville saw a fundamental tension between them. He worried that too much equality would weaken guarantees for individual freedom and minority rights, potentially leading to tyranny. Rousseau, on the other hand, thought that democracy and true freedom require political and moral equality, which require minimal socio-economic quality. Today there are continuing debates in political theory about equality, for example in response to the work of Piketty. In chapter 3, we have seen that AI can impact equality in various ways. The success and legitimacy of democracies also depend on being able to negotiate and balance different political principles, which may be impacted by the way that AI already influences the realization of these values in a non-transparent, non-public way. For example, if democracy requires moral equality, as Rousseau argued, then this is already a sufficient reason to reduce social inequality on these grounds, regardless of other values. If AI increases inequality, for example because it leads to unemployment or increases bias, then according to this reasoning this would be undemocratic since it increases *moral and political* inequality. Yet democracy also requires upholding freedom, including, for example, a sufficient degree of negative freedom. If a redistribution of goods leads to less negative freedom, then one needs to find an acceptable trade-off between freedom and equality. And this balancing act gets even more difficult once we consider various notions of justice, which may not always aim for equality as such, but, for example, for preferential treatment of (presently or previously) disadvantaged groups. Justifications for why AI is undemocratic may thus have to rely on other values such as equality and justice, which can be in tension with one another. Appeals to democracy, in the context of discussions about AI and elsewhere, cannot avoid the difficult politics of such negotiations and balancing acts.

To conclude, what we see here is not only that AI can be used as a tool to directly undermine democracy; it also has unintended side-effects, such as making the ideal of democracy as deliberation more difficult to realize, strengthening populism, threatening public accountability, and increasing power concentration. Moreover, policies concerning AI have to balance different, potentially conflicting political values.

AI and the origins of totalitarianism: Lessons from Arendt

AI and totalitarianism

Democracy can also be defined in contrast to authoritarianism and totalitarianism. The latter not only is authoritarian by having a strong central power that significantly violates democracy in any sense outlined so far (voting, citizen participation, pluralism and diversity, etc.), but also deeply intervenes in the public and private life of its citizens. It is characterized by political repression, censorship, mass surveillance, state terrorism, and the total absence of political liberty. Historical examples of totalitarian regimes are Nazi Germany under Hitler, the Soviet Union under Stalin, Communist China under Mao, and Fascist Italy under Mussolini. Today, digital technologies offer new means for surveillance and manipulation, which may support, or lead to, totalitarianism. AI is one of these technologies. Not only can it help authoritarian rulers and their supporters to rig elections, spread misinformation, and control and repress opposition; it can also help to create a particular kind of surveillance and control: *total* surveillance and *total* control. Bloom (2019) warns of the threat of "totalitarianism 4.0," which leads to a situation in which "everyone will be fully analysed and accounted for. Their every action monitored, their every preference known, their entire life calculated and made predictable" (vii). And if surveillance by means of AI leads to knowledge about everyone, it can then be claimed that AI knows us better than we do. This opens the road to paternalism (chapter 2) and authoritarianism. As McCarthy-Jones (2020) puts it:

> Individualistic western societies are built on the idea that no one knows our thoughts, desires or joys better than we do. [. . .] Artificial intelligence (AI) will change this. It will know us better than we know ourselves. A government armed with AI could claim to know what its people truly want.

McCarthy-Jones compares this idea to what happened in Stalin's Soviet Union and Mao's China. AI enables a digital version of Big Brother, in which every citizen is under constant surveillance by "telescreens." This sounds rather familiar today, especially but not inclusively in states with authoritarian and totalitarian tendencies. Technologically, there is little that stands in the way of mass surveillance by the state using AI and data science. Consider China's social credit system, which is based on digital footprints left by individuals. The state uses video captures by surveillance cameras, facial recognition software, voice recognition, and private data from tech companies such as Alibaba and Baidu. Diamond (2019, 23) calls this a form of "postmodern totalitarianism."

However, AI is not only used to support state totalitarianism; it also enables a kind of corporate totalitarianism. Consider again Zuboff's claim that we live under "surveillance capitalism" (Zuboff 2015; 2019): a new logic of capitalist accumulation that monitors and modifies human behavior. Instead of referring to Big Brother, Zuboff (2015) talks about "Big Other": rather than centralized state control, we face "a ubiquitous networked institutional regime that records, modifies, and commodifies everyday experience from toasters to bodies, communication to thought, all with a view to establishing new pathways to monetization and profit" (81). This may already be happening to some extent via social media, but as the "internet of things" and related technologies transform our homes, workplaces, and cities into smart environments, we can also easily imagine how these may increasingly turn into places where everything is happening under the watchful eye of electronic technology, including AI. And AI does not only watch us, but also makes predictions about our behavior. AI and data science may thus become instruments of new forms of totalitarianism, in which AI knows us better than – and *before* – we do. As Harari has put it in a *WIRED* interview (Thompson, Harari, and Harris 2018), human feelings and human choices are no longer a sacred area. Human beings can now be fully manipulated: "[W]e are now hackable animals." This opens up possibilities for tyranny, by both governments and corporations. Knowledge gained by means of AI and related technologies can be used to manipulate and control us.

Technology thus risks becoming – to pick up a phrase by Arendt (2017) – one of the *origins of totalitarianism*. The shift from democracy to totalitarianism does not happen (just) because a *Führer* or chairman takes over and openly destroys democracy, for example by means of a revolution or coup; rather, the process is much less visible and slower, but not less effective. By means of AI and other electronic technologies, the balance of power is slowly titled into the hands of a few powerful actors – whether in government or in corporations – and certainly away from the people, if they already had much power in the first place. In this way, AI is more than a tool. It is a game changer. As it is applied to the political field, it also changes that field, for example when it contributes to the creation of a totalitarian dynamic.

However, technology is not the only factor that endangers democracy, and its effects certainly do not play out in isolation from the human and social environment in which it operates and is operated. AI alone cannot and should not be blamed for the dangers indicated here. Humans and the social environment, and the ways these interact with the technology, are at least as important. In order to understand that, we need to draw lessons from those who analyzed historical instances of authoritarianism and totalitarianism, who wondered how democracies could deteriorate into their very opposite, and who were motivated by the normative view that what had happened should never happen again. In the previous century, many intellectuals asked precisely these questions after the Second World War, and Arendt was one of them.

Arendt on the origins of totalitarianism and the banality of evil

In *The Origins of Totalitarianism* (2017), originally published in 1951 and written against the background of totalitarianism in Nazi Germany and the Soviet Union, Arendt does not only describe concrete forms of totalitarianism; she also presents an inquiry into the conditions that prepare a society for it. She argues that if totalitarian movements, with "their unsurpassed capacity to establish and safeguard the fictitious world through consistent lying" (499) and their "disdain of the whole texture of reality" (xi), succeeded in establishing a totalitarian transformation of society, it is because there were already conditions in place that prepared modern society for that. She points to the inability of moderns to live in, and make sense of, the world which they made themselves with ever greater power (xi). In particular, she highlights how loneliness – "isolation and lack of normal social relationships" (415) – makes people vulnerable to violent forms of nationalism, which is then used by totalitarian leaders like Hitler. More generally, "terror can rule absolutely only over men who are isolated against each other" (623). Consider Hobbes's reasoning again: only when the lives of individuals are "nasty, brutish, and short," when they are isolated and compete with one another, can the Leviathan establish its authoritarian rule of the sword. The problem is not authoritarianism and totalitarianism as such; there is a deeper wound: the absence of solidarity and collective action, and in the end the destruction of the political sphere itself. As Arendt writes: "Isolation is that impasse into which men are driven when the political sphere of their lives, when they act together in the pursuit of a common concern, is destroyed" (623). It denotes a world without trust, a world "where nobody is reliable and nothing can be relied upon" (628).

Today the phenomenon of movements that shield themselves and their followers "from the impact of factuality" (Arendt 2017, 549) sounds rather familiar when we consider Trumpism, fake news, and (non-governmental) terrorism, as does the talk of loneliness and the inability to make sense of the world. This is not only a problem of the less well educated or those who are excluded from society. Many Trump supporters are middle class (Rensch 2019). And surely not all of them are or were lonely in the sense of being alone or having no friends. But they can be seen as *politically* lonely in Arendt's sense, lacking a world of solidarity and trust. While acknowledging the relevance of issues such as bias, exploitation, and neo-colonialism (see chapters 3 and 5) and the role of populist and right-wing propaganda and ideology, one could argue that in the US today, political isolation and a world devoid of trust help to form an ideal soil for the rise of authoritarianism. If Arendt is right, authoritarianism and totalitarianism do not so much *create* a damaged social fabric as grow on one that is *already* damaged. Viewed from an Arendtian angle, totalitarianism is, strictly speaking, not a political movement but a movement that destroys the political sphere itself. It is not just anti-democratic in the sense of authoritarian, but also "organized loneliness" (Arendt 2017, 628), the destruction of trust in each other, and the corrosion of the belief in truth and facts. In this light, we must ask again the question concerning technology: can and do contemporary technologies such as AI contribute to these conditions, and if so, how?

AI can certainly be used in order to shield people from reality or create a distortion of reality, for example when it creates the epistemic bubbles previously mentioned or straightforwardly spreads misinformation. But it may also contribute to the underlying psychosocial and social-epistemic conditions for totalitarianism mentioned by Arendt. One version of this argument could be made by focusing on literal loneliness (thus differing somewhat from Arendt). According to Turkle, machines can contribute to loneliness as they give us only the illusion of companionship. In *Alone Together* (2011), she writes that robots "may offer the illusion of companionship without the demands of friendship" (1). We are networked but feel "utterly alone" (154). We might no longer take the risk of friendship with humans, since we fear the dependence that comes with it (66). We hide behind the screen. Even calling other people is seen as too direct. But if we do this, we miss out on human empathy and on taking care of one another. We miss out on responding to each other's needs. We miss out on real friendship and love. And we risk treating others as objects, using them for our comfort or amusement (154). How big these risks are and whether they are created by social media is contested; Turkle may well be too dismissive of the positive social possibilities offered by the technology. But the danger of being "alone together" needs to be taken seriously. If Arendt is right, this loneliness is not only a sad state at the personal level; if it leads to a general loss of trust and solidarity, it is also a *political* problem and dangerous to the extent that it helps to create a ground for totalitarianism.

Insofar as AI and other digital technologies contribute to these phenomena, they are also politically problematic. Consider, for example, how social media create anxiety and may result in tribalization: we are constantly bombarded by sensational bad news and only trust information from our "tribe" (Javanbakht 2020). Echo chambers and epistemic bubbles further contribute to this tribalization. Anxiety exacerbates loneliness and separation, and tribalization may not only result in political polarization and distribution of the public sphere, but also lead to violence. In addition, when Arendt (2017, 573–4) claims that the Nazi concentration camps transformed human persons into mere things in scientifically controlled ways, one could also consider how contemporary forms of behavioral manipulation through AI may have a similar moral impact insofar as they turn people into what Arendt calls "perverted" animals, open for hacking. Consider again surveillance capitalism and how the data economy is based on the exploitation and manipulation of people. And there are more parallels with the atrocities that happened in the Second World War and, more generally, with the evils of totalitarianism. In *Privacy is Power* (2020), Carissa Véliz compares the scenario of a contemporary authoritarian regime getting hold of our personal data to the use of registries by the Nazis for mass murdering Jews (115). As she puts it: "[D]ata collection can kill" (114). AI and data science can be used for such purposes and, less visibly, create the *conditions* for such phenomena.

Yet it is never technology on its own that kills or installs and maintains a totalitarian regime. People are also needed: in particular, people who obey orders; people who do not resist. And this leads us to another book by Arendt: *Eichmann in Jerusalem* (2006), famous for its subtitle: "A Report on the Banality of Evil." Writing in 1963, Arendt analyzes the trial two years earlier of Adolf Eichmann, a Nazi who played a major role in the mass murder of Jews during the Second World War. Arendt herself witnessed the trial. The report provoked a lot of reactions. Instead of seeing Eichmann as a monster or hater of Jews, Arendt took seriously his own view that he followed orders: "[H]e would have had a bad conscience only if he had not done what he had been ordered to do" (25). He did his "duty" (135) in the sense of obeying orders and following the law of Nazi Germany, which meant following the orders of the *Führer*. There could be no exceptions (137); it was a "virtue" to be obedient

(247). This analysis contributed to Arendt's project of inquiring into the origins of totalitarianism: she concluded that obedience, not resisting, is part of the evil involved. Nazi Germany could not have committed its crimes and atrocities without the many people who, like Eichmann, "just" followed orders and pursued their career. This is the banal, ordinary face of the totalitarian evil, but one which is no less "fearsome" (252). For Arendt, this obedience was more important than the inner life and motives of the totalitarian leaders (278). Yet she is hopeful that there will always be some who resist: "[U]nder conditions of terror most people will comply but some people will not" (233).

For understanding the relation between AI and totalitarianism, this means that we should not only look at the intentions and motives of people (which may be good, bad – e.g., intending to manipulate people in order to seize power – or banal – e.g., making a career in an AI company as a data scientist), but also consider the unintended consequences and how *just doing your job* may contribute to these. Usually, bias is not intended. For example, it is highly likely that a particular team of developers and data scientists do not *intend* to increase bias in society. But by doing their job within a larger corporation or governmental organization, they might do exactly that. While there *may* be a small number of people with bad intentions (in tech companies or elsewhere), generally this is not the case; rather, just doing your job and obeying authority may lead to the creation or proliferation of bias. From an Arendtian perspective, the bad or evil is in not questioning, not thinking, just doing what one is supposed to do. It is located in the banality of people doing their "duty" in everyday technological practices and the related hierarchical structures. The evil is in the moment of compliance when non-compliance is needed to avoid a bad or evil outcome. Or, politically speaking: it is in the moment of not resisting when resistance is the right thing to do.

Resistance is not only important under totalitarianism; it is also important in a democracy. In part, the possibility of disobedience is enshrined in the legal framework itself. As Hildebrandt (2015) argues, "[D]isobedience and contestability are the hallmarks of law in a constitutional democracy" (10). In a democracy with the rule of law, citizens can contest norms and their application. But with Arendt one could go further and argue, more controversially, that *regardless* of what a (court of) law says, resistance may be justified and required on moral and political grounds. In any case, Arendt's point that *blindly* following rules and orders is very dangerous and morally problematic is also relevant in democracies.

A related argument points at the lack of *thinking*. Inspired by *Eichmann in Jerusalem*, McQuillan (2019) argues that since AI offers people "empirical rankings of risk, whose derivation they have no way of questioning," the technology "encourages thoughtlessness in the sense described by Hannah Arendt: the inability to critique instructions, the lack of reflection on consequences, a commitment to the belief that a correct ordering is being carried out" (165). The danger of a statistical approach promoted by AI is also that, to the extent that it is based on historical data, we get more of the same, we remain stuck in the old. In *The Human Condition* (1958), Arendt writes:

> The new always happens against the overwhelming odds of statistical laws and their probability, which for all practical, everyday purposes amounts to certainty; the new therefore always appears in the guise of a miracle. The fact that man is capable of action means that the unexpected can be expected from him, that he is able to perform what is infinitely improbable. (178)

While McQuillan's way of seeing AI sounds too deterministic and risks unnecessarily assuming a strict opposition between humans and technology (humans also play a role), there is a significant danger that specific uses of AI – that is, specific combinations of AI and humans – contribute to shaping the conditions under which totalitarianism can grow and flourish.

The point about conditions is important. In order to avoid AI totalitarianism (and to maintain democracy), it is not sufficient to point to the responsibility of people in tech companies and governmental organizations and say that they should improve the design of the technology, the data, and so on. It is also necessary to ask the questions: what kind of social environment could be created that supports people to exercise this responsibility and makes it easier for them to question, criticize, or even resist when resistance is the right thing to do? What barriers can be created to hinder the described shifts from democracy to totalitarianism? And how can we create the conditions under which *democracy* can flourish?

The answer to these questions, of course, depends on the ideal of democracy (and politics); in this chapter, I have given an overview of some of these ideals and the tensions between them. But more work is needed to dig into the conditions that make democracy work. Here philosophy and the sciences (and the arts!) can collaborate. For example, inspired by Miessen and Ritt's (2019) volume on the spatial politics of right-wing populism, we may ask about the spatial and material conditions for democracy. What spaces would be good for democratic deliberation? And what kind of spaces could AI produce? How could AI help to create good architectures for democracy, literally and metaphorically? What kind of *agora* and public space do we need, not only conceptually but also very concretely, materially, and spatially? And what is the relation between, on the one hand, the political and the social and, on the other hand, material artifacts? For example, I have asked elsewhere (Coeckelbergh 2009a) what it would mean to speak of a "politics of artifacts": I questioned Arendt's anthropocentric definition of the *polis* in *The Human Condition*, which assumes a strict distinction between humans and artifacts, but highlighted the importance of political events (the launch of Sputnik in her prologue) and retrieved the idea that for a public realm we need a common world that gathers us together, perhaps including somehow a "community of things" (Arendt 1958, 52–5). In chapter 6, I will further discuss the idea of including non-humans within the political sphere and the role of hybridity in politics. More generally, we need to know more about the precise relations between, on the one hand, politics and the social and, on the other hand knowledge, space, and material technologies. We need to think through the conditions for democracy and the building of the public sphere in the light of new technologies and technological environments.

One way that political philosophy and philosophy of technology can contribute to this project is by conceptualizing power and – much less understood – its relation to technology. If we want to better understand what we are doing together and what we *could* do together in the light of technologies such as AI (not just the dangers but also the opportunities), we need to understand how power works and how it relates to knowledge and technology. This is the topic of the next chapter.

5

Power: Surveillance and (Self-) Disciplining by Data

Introduction: Power as a topic in political philosophy

One way to talk about politics is to use the concept of power. Power is often seen in negative terms or as a representation of how things really are as opposed to an ideal. For example, power has been invoked in response to those who defend deliberative and participative ideals of liberal democracy. Consider Dewey's ideal of participative democracy again. Critics have argued that this ideal is naïve since it avoids talking about conflict and power. In particular, it is deemed to be too optimistic about the capacity of ordinary citizens to judge and act intelligently and about the chances to reach consensus, thereby ignoring what Hildreth (2009) calls the "darker forces in human nature, including a thirst for power and the willingness to manipulate social relations to one's advantage" (781). Not so long after Dewey, Mills wrote in *The Power Elite* (1956) that American society is ruled by people in corporations, the military, and the government who "are in command of the major hierarchies and organizations of modern society" (4) and have access to the power and wealth available there. Instead of citizens "held in responsible check by a plurality of voluntary associations which connect debating publics with the pinnacles of decisions," as defenders of participative democracy may imagine things should work, Mills saw a "system of organized irresponsibility" (361) run by an elite. Public problem-solving as Dewey imagined it does not work on a large scale. Politics requires the fight for power, and cannot be modeled on scientific models of problem-solving. Dewey mistakenly ignored how power is distributed in society and how deeply divided societies can be. As we have seen in the previous chapter, this criticism is also in line with Mouffe and Rancière, who propose to instead examine power as dissensus and agonism. And Marxism questions the power distribution between social classes, emphasizing how capital gives power to those who own it. In both cases, power is linked to struggle, which can be used productively under specific conditions.

Another example of power versus ideals, which is directly relevant to AI, is power versus freedom as consent. In the United States and in Europe, clicking that you agree to a particular internet platform's terms of service – including its data processing policy and hence the way AI is put to work – is meant to protect the rights of consumers, including their freedom. However, as Bietti (2020) has argued, this regulatory device fails to account for the unjust background conditions and power structures under which these individual consent acts take place. If power imbalances are "shaping the environment in which a decision to consent is made," then consent is "an empty construct" (315). Power is also seen as a danger to truth (Lukes 2019) and potentially deceptive. Power can be used for coercion, for example in the context of a totalitarian state. But it can also take the form of various forms of manipulation. This threatens reasoning and the development of critical capacities. Thinking is also difficult when you are constantly in a competitive environment where you cannot afford the time to slow down (Berardi 2017). Power is then seen as the enemy of thinking itself.

Yet power is not necessarily bad. An influential and arguably more complex view of power is offered by Foucault. Inspired by Nietzsche, Foucault (1981, 93–4) conceptualized society in terms of power, in particular force relations. But his view differs considerably from Marxism. Instead of analyzing power top down, in terms of centralized sovereignty and the power of rulers or elites, he proposes a bottom-up approach starting from the small mechanisms and operations of power that shape subjects, produce particular kinds of bodies, and pervade the whole of society. He analyzes these micro-mechanisms of power in prisons and hospitals. Instead of linking power to the head of Leviathan, the central authoritarian sovereign in Hobbes's thinking, Foucault (1980) focuses on the plurality and the body of power: on "the myriad of bodies which are constituted as peripheral subjects as a result of the effects of power" (98), on power's "infinitesimal mechanisms" (99). Power is exercised within the social body "rather than from above it" (39); it "circulates" (98) through the social body (119). Moreover, Foucault is interested in how power "reaches into the very grain of individuals, touches their bodies and inserts itself into their actions and attitudes, their discourses, learning processes and everyday lives" (39). Individuals are not only the points on which power works; instead, they simultaneously exercise and undergo power; they are "the vehicles of power, not its points of application" (98). The individual is the effect of power.

What do these different views of power imply for the politics of AI? Is AI used by those who manipulate social relations to their advantage and deceive us? And how does it interact with the micro-mechanisms of power that Foucault describes? What kind of individuals, subjects, and bodies are made by means of AI? In this chapter, I ask these questions and apply political and social theory of power to AI. First, I will use a general conceptual framework about power and technology as developed by Sattarov in order to distinguish between various ways AI may impact power. Then I will draw on three theories of power in order to elaborate on some relations between AI and power: Marxism and critical theory, Foucault and Butler, and a performance-oriented approach as proposed in my own work. This will lead to a conclusion about what I will call "artificial power" (the initial title of this book).

Power and AI: Towards a general conceptual framework

The relation between politics and technology is by now a well-known topic in contemporary philosophy of technology. Consider Winner's (1980) work, which shows that technologies can have unintended political consequences, and Feenberg's (1991) critical theory of technology, which is not only inspired by Marx and critical theory (in particular Marcuse) but also empirically oriented. However, while elsewhere there is much interest in *power*, for example in cultural studies, gender studies, posthumanism, and so on, there have been few systematic philosophical treatments and overviews of the topic in philosophy of technology. In ethics of computing there is work on the power of algorithms (Lash 2007; Yeung 2016), but a systematic framework to think about power and technology was lacking for decades. An exception is Sattarov's *Power and Technology* (2019), which distinguishes between different conceptions of power and applies them to technology. While his contribution is mainly geared towards technology ethics, rather than political philosophy of technology, it is very helpful for the purpose of analyzing the relations between AI and power.

Sattarov distinguishes between four conceptions of power. The first conception, which he calls *episodic*, is about relationships in which one actor exercises power over another, for instance by means of seduction, coercion, or manipulation. The second conception defines power as a *disposition*: as a capacity, ability, or potential. The third, systematic conception, understands power as a property of social and political *institutions*. The fourth conception sees power as *constituting or producing* the social actors themselves (Sattarov 2019, 100). The latter two are thus more structural, whereas the first are about actors and their actions (13).

Following Sattarov, we can map these different conceptions of power onto relations between power and technology. First, technology can (help to) seduce, coerce, force, or manipulate people, and can be used to exercise authority. One could also say that this kind of power is delegated to the technology or – to pick up a concept that is often used in postphenomenology of technology – that the technology mediates. For example, online advertisements can seduce users to visit a website, speed bumps can force drivers to slow down, and technology can also manipulate. Technology can "nudge": it can change the choice architecture so that people are more likely to behave in certain ways, without them being aware of this (see also chapter 2). Second, technology can give power to people in the sense that it increases their abilities and potential for action; it can *em*power. This is also true for humanity in general, as Jonas (1984) has argued: technology has given humanity enormous power.

Consider the concept of the Anthropocene: humanity as a whole has become a kind of geological force (Crutzen 2006). It has acquired a hyper agency that has transformed the entire surface of the earth (see also the next chapter). Third, when it comes to systemic power, we can see how technology can support particular systems and ideologies. For example, from a Marxian view, technology supports the advancement of capitalism. Power here is not about what individuals do; rather, it is embedded in a particular political, economic, or social system, to which technology contributes. For example, mass media shape public opinion. This is also true for social media, which may support a particular political-economic system (e.g., capitalism). Finally, if power is not just something that is possessed or exercised by individuals, or applied to individuals, but is also constitutive of subjects, selves, and identities, as Foucault has argued, then technology can be used to constitute such subjects, selves, and identities. Often there is no intention on the part of technology developers and users to do this, but it may happen nevertheless. For example, social media may shape your identity, even if you are not aware of it.

What does this mean for thinking about power and AI?

First, AI can seduce, coerce, or manipulate, for example via social media and recommender systems. Like algorithms in general (Sattarov 2019, 100), AI can be designed to change the attitude and behaviors of users. Without using coercion, it can function as a "persuasive technology" (Fogg 2003) by seducing and manipulating people. Music recommender systems such as Spotify or sites like Amazon aim to steer the listening or buying behavior of people by nudging them through changing the decision environment (see also the previous chapters), for example by suggesting that other people with a similar taste in books have bought book x and book y. And the order of Facebook posts is decided by an algorithm, which can, for example, influence the feelings of users through processes of "contagion" (Papacharissi 2015). Individuals are clustered into groups based on similar interests and behavior, which may reproduce social stereotypes and reaffirm old power structures (Bartoletti 2020). People are also manipulated by means of dynamic pricing and other "personalization" techniques, exploiting individual decision-making vulnerabilities, including well-known biases (Susser, Roessler, and Nissenbaum 2019, 12).

As in all forms of manipulation, people are influenced to act in a certain way without them being aware of this influencing. As we have seen, such covert influencing of individuals' decision-making threatens freedom, understood as individual autonomy. To the extent that this happens, we are no longer in control of our choices, and do not even understand the underlying mechanisms of how this happens. While the modern conception of autonomy, according to which we are or should be atomistic and rationalistic individuals, is not adequate and has been criticized inside and outside mainstream Western philosophy (see, e.g., discussions about relational autonomy in Christman 2004 and Westlund 2009), even as social and relational beings we want some control over our decisions and our lives, and we do not want to be manipulated. In terms of power, the mentioned forms of seduction and manipulation by AI shift the power balance (even more) to those who collect, own, and monetize our data. Moreover, particular groups in society (e.g., racist groups) may try to gain power by manipulating people on social media.

Second, AI may empower by increasing people's individual capacities. Consider, for example, natural language processing that helps translate and thus opens up new possibilities for individuals (as well as creating problems, e.g., deskilling and threats to privacy). But AI also increases the potential for exercising power over others, humans and non-humans, and in the end it increases humanity's power over the natural environment and the earth. Consider, for instance, search engines and social media, which may empower individuals who previously did not have access to this amount and bandwidth of information, and who might not have had a voice in classic media. But at the same time those search engines and the companies who offer them are given a lot of power: they shape information flows and hence play what is known as a gatekeeper role. In addition, the companies and their algorithms use personalization: they "filter information per individual," which introduces human and technical biases (Bozdag 2013, 1). This gatekeeping role and these biases have implications for democracy and diversity (Granka 2010). As we already saw in chapter 3, in terms of power, AI serves here the interests of some people rather than others. AI can also be used at the level of the state to enable surveillance and its authoritarian use. It offers governments and their intelligence agencies power in the sense of new instruments and capacities for surveillance, which can lead to enhanced oppression and even totalitarianism. Sometimes states and private companies team up to increase those capacities, as in China and the US. The corporate tech sector knows a lot about the lives of citizens (Couldry and Meijas 2019, 13). Even liberal democracies are installing facial recognition systems, use predictive policing, and employ AI tools at their borders. There is the risk that what Sætra (2020, 4) calls a new form of "algorithmic governance" will order "human action in general." Moreover, AI also empowers humanity as a whole, which may have consequences for non-humans such as animals and for natural environments. If, in the context of the Anthropocene, AI further increases humanity's ability to intervene in, and transform, nature, then it further supports an ongoing shift in terms of power: from non-humans to humans. Consider AI that helps to extract natural resources from the earth and the energy consumption by AI technology (see chapter 6), which in turn also requires the use of natural resources. That AI affords power to humans may be empowering at the individual level, but may have vast consequences for non-human nature, given the increased Baconian powers of humanity to mine and transform the earth: scientific knowledge and technologies are used to control nature. In the next chapter, I will say more about these non-human and earthly aspects of the politics and power of AI.

Third, AI can support neoliberal versions of capitalism, authoritarianism, and other systems and ideologies. Software and hardware systems related to AI "form part of the broader social, economic, and political institutional reality" (Sattarov 2019, 102), and this includes socio-economic systems and ideologies. Those larger systems affect the development of technology, for example by creating a context of investment in AI, but technology may also help to maintain those systems. For example, Dyer-Witheford, Kjøsen, and Steinhoff (2019) claim that AI is an instrument of capital, and therefore entails exploitation and the concentration of power in the hands of the owners of high tech – who are in turn concentrated in particular countries and regions such as the US (Nemitz 2018). Thus, AI is not just technological but also creates or maintains a particular social order, here capitalism and neoliberalism. Consider also again Zuboff's claim about surveillance capitalism: the point is not only that a particular technology is problematic; AI and big data help to create, maintain, and expand an entire socio-economic system in which capital is accumulated (by some) through technologies that harvest and sell data (of the many), thus exploiting human nature and reaching into the intimate sphere. Even our emotions are monitored and monetized (McStay 2018). The same AI technology can be used to support totalitarian regimes or to maintain oppressive political systems and their corresponding narratives and images (e.g., a racist utopia), although in principle AI could also offer opportunities for supporting democracy – much depends on how we think of democracy (see chapter 4) and indeed about politics.

Most researchers in AI and the politics of AI support a democratic and fair way of coding. Some believe we need more limits and regulation. Oppressive effects are not always and not usually intended, although sometimes AI is used on purpose to promote a racist and nationalist politics. Yet as we have seen in chapter 3 and 4, there are also problematic non-intended effects. AI may support racist and neo-colonial political cultures and systems by introducing bias against particular individuals and groups, or help to create the conditions for authoritarianism or totalitarianism. Consider again Noble's (2018) argument that (search) algorithms and classification systems may "reinforce oppressive social relationships" (1). An example of such "algorithmic oppression" (4) was the case of Google Photos that tagged African Americans as "apes" and "animals" – a problem Google could not really fix (Simonite 2018). However, whether a particular use or outcome of AI is biased or unjust is not always as clear as in this case, and also depends on one's conceptions of justice and equality (see chapter 3). In any case, decisions, thoughts, actions, and emotions can also be controlled on purpose in order to support a particular political system. In the case of totalitarianism, AI may support the system's unlimited reach into the minds and hearts of people.

Fourth, AI can play a role in the constitution of the self and the formation of the subject, even if we are not aware of it. The point here is not only that AI manipulates us and intervenes deeply at the personal level in the sense that it can help to deduce the thoughts and feelings of people – making inferences about their inner states based on observable behaviors such as facial expressions and musical preferences, which are then used for predication and monetization by surveillance capitalism – but also that AI contributes to the shaping of how we understand and experience ourselves. While what Rouvroy (2013) calls "algorithmic governmentality" bypasses "any encounter with human reflexive subjects" (144), does not allow room for human judgments and explicit evaluations of our beliefs and ourselves, and leads to exploitation of relations between individuals (Stiegler 2019), this does not mean that there is no effect on our self(-knowledge). What kind of perception and knowledge of the self does AI help to create? For example, do we start to understand ourselves as producers and collections of data for sale? Do we quantify ourselves and our lives as we track ourselves and are tracked by others? Do we think that we have "data doubles" (Lyon 2014), digital models of ourselves – even if AI does not store a digital model of the user (Matzner 2019)? Do we acquire and communicate a networked sense of self (Papacharissi 2011)? What sort of identity and subjectivity is enabled by AI?

Asking such questions goes beyond an instrumentalist understanding of human–technology relations. The self and human subjectivity are not external to information technologies such as AI; instead, "digital technology does something to human subjectivity itself" (Matzner 2019, 109). AI technologies have impacted the way we perceive and act in the world, leading to new forms of subjectivity (118). And there are different forms of subjectivity connected to AI. For example, based on the kinds of subjects we are and the kind of communities we belong to, we will react differently to a particular AI-based security system. If someone is not recognized by the system, this may be perceived as threatening by one person, given personal previous experiences and tensions in a particular social context (e.g., racism that has impacted that person and community), whereas another person from another background might have fewer problems with it. In Matzner's (2019) words: "[S]pecific applications of AI connect in quite different manners to pre-existing sociotechnical situations and the respective forms of subjectivity" (109). AI technology will enable different relations to different subjectivities because we are situated subjects (118). In line with Foucault's view, this means that the power of AI is not just about (top-down) manipulations, capacities, and systems; it is also about concrete, situated experiences and mechanisms of power, shaped by the technology. One could also say (as I will do at the end of this chapter): as living, moving, and situated beings, we *perform* self and power, and AI plays a role in these performances, for example by co-directing them.

Let me further unpack this framework for thinking about AI and power by focusing on three theoretical directions. A first, perhaps obvious, theoretical resource for framing, understanding, and evaluating AI's impact on power is Marxism. Then I will further elaborate the idea that AI makes us into subjects by using Foucault, and develop the claim that power is performed – through technology.

Marxism: AI as a tool for technocapitalism

From a Marxian point of view, the power of AI is conceptualized in terms of support for capitalism and a particular social class. By means of AI, big tech and other capitalists rule us. We are living under a new form of what Suarez-Villa (2009) calls "technocapitalism": corporations, in their "quest for power and profit" (2), try to control not only all aspects of the public domain but also our lives (see Zuboff's argument about surveillance capitalism again). Furthermore, AI is used in the service of capitalist states and their nationalist agendas. Bartoletti (2020) compares AI with nuclear power: AI is used for a new international arms race. One could add that AI is also similar to nuclear power in the sense that – according to this kind of argument at least – by means of AI, power is exercised top down from a central position and in an undemocratic way. Just as most of us have never been asked if we wanted nuclear power, we have never been asked if we wanted AI surveillance and biometrics, AI decision systems, AI that processes data from our phone, and so on. Towards individual citizens, AI is power in the sense that it enables dominance and, for some more than others, oppression. The data economy is political and power-full through and through.

However, there is no such thing as "AI" oppressing us, as if the technology would operate on its own. AI should not be understood as an isolated factor or atomistic artificial agent; it is always connected to humans, and the impact of AI on power happens always with and through humans. If AI can be said to "have" power at all (e.g., power over humans), it is power *through* humans and through society. From a Marxian point of view, it is living labor, not the machines themselves, that produces surplus value for the capitalists (Harvey 2019, 109). Moreover, AI and roboticization aim to replace human labor. As Harvey (2019) puts it: "Robots do not (except in science fiction accounts) complain, answer back, sue, get sick, go slow, lose concentration, go on strike, demand more wages, worry about work conditions, want tea breaks or simply fail to show up" (121–2). Even so-called "immaterial" labor (Lazzarato 1996; see also Hardt and Negri 2000) that produces software or virtual worlds requires humans. Furthermore, political choices about AI are made by governments and those who develop and employ it. AI and data science are political and power-full in the sense that in the context of a data economy, decisions are made by people and about people at every level and in every stage, in invisible ways:

> The choice about which data sets are studied is being made by people. It is a subjective decision, and a political one. Each individual, once entered into a data set, becomes part of a new trans-action between them and the unseen force that has put them into it, and has used that data set to train an algorithm and ultimately make a decision about them. This represents an asymmetry of power, and this asymmetry – the outcome of choice and power – is what underpins the politics of data and, ultimately, the data economy. The data economy is political at every level, not least because some organizations hold a huge amount of power over others by deciding who gets onto a data set, and who is left out, a decision that may have far-reaching implications. (Bartoletti 2020, 38)

To acknowledge the politics and power of AI in terms of the "many hands" involved in its operations does not mean that there is no centralized and top-down use of power. Both corporations and governments use AI in a centralized way. As we have seen in the previous chapter, this can take the form of technocracy. Sætra (2020) defends this: prioritizing the public interest, AI can achieve a form of rational optimization, and most problems, properly understood, are "technical problems amenable to the logical of statistical analysis and optimization" (2). Against this view, one could argue – in line with environmental philosophy and (I add) philosophy of technology – that technical issues are also political, and that humans, as political animals and moral agents who can have compassion and wisdom, need to be involved and accountable (5–7). Yet Sætra nevertheless believes that if AI were further developed, it could possibly solve complex issues for us, since it would be better than humans in creating and identifying the best policies, especially when it comes to areas such as science, engineering, and complex societal and macroeconomic issues (5). However, one could object that these issues are also political, and that politics cannot and should not be dealt with in an exclusively technocratic way, since this violates the principle of democracy and since human judgment is needed in politics (see the previous chapter).

Yet these arguments could be made without reference to capitalism. From a specific Marxian point of view, the main problem is not so much technocracy and lack of democracy as such, but a specific socio-economic system with a logic of its own. For example, Dyer-Witheford, Kjøsen, and Steinhoff (2019) observe that today capitalism is "possessed" by the AI question and argue that AI is an instrument of capital and exploitation. AI does not only have a technological logic but also a social one, in particular the logic of producing surplus value. It contributes to the creation and maintenance of a particular social order: a capitalist one (1–2). AI replaces work, and if it doesn't, it intensifies the work and the threat of replacement helps to intimidate workers. People are made disposable or are made to feel that they are (5). While some socialists see AI as an opportunity to create a different society, for example by means of universal basic income, Dyer-Witheford, Kjøsen, and Steinhoff focus on the problems: new forms of exploitation and the looming prospect of capitalism without humans.

Yet what AI does to human beings is not limited to the sphere of production and labor, narrowly defined. AI becomes part of production but also extracts knowledge and shapes our cognition and emotions. From affective computing (Picard 1997) to affective AI, digital technologies intervene at the personal, intimate, and emotional level. "Emotional AI" (McStay 2018) is used for discerning emotional states, sentiment analysis, and measuring happiness. For example, companies may use sentiment analysis to recognize, monitor, and manipulate affective states of people: this is a form of cognitive but also affective capitalism (Karppi et al. 2016). These "operations aimed at your person-ality, moods, and emotions, your lies and vulnerabilities" (Zuboff 2019, 199), lead to new forms of exploitation, domination, and political manipulation, for example data-driven campaigning (see Simon 2019; Tufekci 2018). Social media also favor emotionally engaged messages: affective contagion (Sampson 2012) is used to influence crowds. This may increase extremism and populism, perhaps even lead to violence and war.

The manipulation of emotions for political purposes evokes long-standing philosophical discussions about "the passions," "affect," "emotions," and so on, from Spinoza to today's philosophy and cognitive science, including discussions about the role of emotions in politics and related questions such as: what is the role of the body in politics and what is the "body politic"? Is our ability to be affected our weak spot, politically speaking? For example, Hardt (2015) has argued that the power to be affected is not necessarily a weakness and that we are non-sovereign subjects. From this point of view, perhaps anger could play a positive role in politics. Nussbaum (2016), by contrast, argues against people who believe that caring about justice needs anger: it is normatively inappropriate (7) and instead we need generosity and impartial welfare institutions. A more positive view of the role of "the passions" in politics is offered by Farkas and Schou (2020), who, as we have seen in chapter 4, argue that politics and democracy are not just about facts, reason, and evidence, but also about clashes of different positions and "about affect, emotions and feelings" (7). Emotions are therefore needed in a vibrant version of democracy as Mouffe imagines it (see chapter 4). One could then discuss what the role of AI is vis-à-vis such conditions. This contrasts with the view that ordinary citizens are too emotional to engage in democratic debate, and that we need either technocracy or rationalistic education of citizens, rather than emotions. Another controversial topic that concerns emotions and politics is belonging: the feeling of belonging is important, perhaps, but can lead to nationalism and populism – the rise of which is also influenced by AI (see the previous chapter). The way AI impacts on the emotional aspects of politics, capitalism, and democracy needs further investigation.

When it comes to taking a critical perspective on AI and power, "data colonialism" (Couldry and Mejias 2019) is another term that has been used to express that the exploitation of humans and human lives by means of AI is unacceptable from a critical theory perspective. The appropriation of data is then understood through the history of colonialism: just as historical colonialism appropriated territory and resources for profit, data colonialism exploits human beings through the appropriation of data (Couldry and Mejias 2019). Colonialism is also invoked in discussions about AI and bias, as we saw in chapter 3.

Nudging can also be seen as problematic from a critical theory point of view: the fact that it is a more subtle way of manipulation does not make it less exploitative, since it is used for making profit in a capitalist manner and context. And as already indicated in chapter 2, nudging is also problematic for other reasons: it bypasses the human capacity for autonomous decision-making and judgment. AI increases these possibilities for nudging. Yeung (2016) shows that algorithmic decision-guidance techniques are used to shape the choice context in which individual decision-making occurs. She talks about "hypernudges" since these nudges are continually updated and pervasive, which has troubling implications for democracy and human flourishing. But nudging is not only problematic because of its direct influence on particular human beings; it also involves a certain way of seeing human beings, which enables the specific manipulative and exploitative relations that are so troubling. In their criticism of Floridi's (2014) idea that we are informational organisms or inforgs, Couldry and Mejias (2019) write that when we are (made into) inforgs, then we are open to manipulation and modulation: "Inforgs are the perfect creatures for the hypernudge to rule when they have been refashioned to always be open to data flows and so continuously available for modulation" (158). And if we think of such inforgs as science fiction, then it is good to be aware that, like human emotions and heuristics, science fiction is also used by capitalism to support its system (Canavan 2015; Eshun 2003). Or can it also be used to critique capitalist agendas and operations, empower citizens, and suggest resistance?

The Marxian way of framing and analyzing issues concerning AI and power leads to the question whether there is a way to resist, transform, or overthrow capitalism. As a general question, this has been discussed since Marx, and as a topic on its own, it is beyond the scope of this book. With regard to AI, it is worth noting that some critical theory scholars discern the possibility of aligning AI with ideals of social justice and egalitarianism and bringing about a structural renewal, withdrawing power from hegemonic institutions (McQuillan 2019, 170). Yet seeing AI as an instrument for resistance or revolution could face considerable challenges, given that similar hopes and claims were made regarding the internet. As Castells (2001) and others have shown, first the internet was born in the military-industrial complex, then hackers saw it as a space for liberation, experimentation, and even a kind of virtual communitarianism (although today libertarianism seems to have triumphed in Silicon Valley). The internet has indeed a kind of openness and promises a more "horizontal" structure of power. It also has restructured labor and social class, to some extent at least. Dyer-Witheford (2015) shows that the people who work for the tech industry do not fit neatly into classes. The hacker ethic seems empowering and has potential for resistance to capitalist hegemony. For example, as Castells (2001, 139) writes, hackers can disrupt the websites of government agencies or corporations seen as oppressive or exploitative. But there is also criticism: generally, the use of information technology and its developers are compliant with corporate and military priorities (Dyer-Witheford 2015, 62–3). Many fear that AI is also going in that direction: instead of a tool of social transformation, it may well become one of oppression and exploitation. Democratization of AI is sometimes advocated by big tech, but at the same time it is unwilling to restrict its power and does not accept external intervention (Sudmann 2019, 25). A tension remains between what it proclaims and what it actually does. While AI research is often driven by idealism, when embedded in corporations, competition seems to prevail (Sudmann 2019, 24) and AI and algorithms may contribute to growing social inequality, for example in the US (Noble 2018). Finally, it has been argued that science-fiction scenarios about AI seem to help to maintain, rather than question, the dominant socio-economic system: capitalism. As Harvey (2019) puts it: "New technologies (like the internet and social media) promise a utopian socialist future but get co-opted by capital into new forms and modes of exploitation and accumulation in the absence of other forms of action" (113). Note, however, that there are socio-economic systems, for example in Europe, in which AI capitalism is subordinated, at least to some extent, to ethical and political norms of democratic societies.

Foucault: How AI subjects us and makes us into subjects

Not everyone agrees with the Marxian view of power or with the view that power is something that is exercised centrally. In his influential work on the topic, Foucault argued that power is not (just) about a sovereign political authority wielding power, but that it is implicated in all social relations and institutions. Moreover, he was critical of what he saw as Marxism's "economism" in its theory of power (Foucault 1980, 88): there is more than economic power. While it is true that power serves "the reproduction of the relations of production," thus maintaining class domination, power serves also other functions and "passes through much finer channels" (72). As I already explained in the introduction to this chapter, according to Foucault, power pervades the whole of society and reaches down into individual subjects and their bodies in various contexts and ways, which are not limited to the economic domain. Furthermore, Foucault thinks that selves and subjects are *made* and make themselves, and that this is also a form of power. Let us now take a closer look at these views.

Disciplining and surveillance

First, Foucault argued that power comes in the form of disciplining and surveillance. In *Discipline and Punish*, he shows that under modern disciplinary power, individuals are used as objects and instruments (Foucault 1977, 170): the body is rendered docile, obedient, and useful. Based on this framework, one could argue that through AI-powered social media, surveillance technologies, and so on, docile bodies are created. The attention economy of social media makes us into scrolling and clicking machines and people are put under surveillance in airports and other border control environments. AI also contributes to the creation of a new kind of panopticon (Fuchs et al. 2012). Designed by the English philosopher Jeremy Bentham in the 18th century, the panopticon was initially a type of prison architecture in the form of a central observation tower placed within a circle of prison cells. From the tower, the guards can see every prisoner but the prisoners cannot see into the tower, which means they never know if they are being watched. As a disciplinary concept, the panopticon applies to the idea that people behave as if they are watched, without knowing whether that is the case. This is a more subtle form of control: it is a kind of self-regulation and a "political technology" (Downing 2008, 82–3). For Foucault (1980), panopticism constituted a new way that power was exercised: it was "a technological invention in the order of power" (71). He referred to Bentham's prison design, but today AI can be understood as contributing to all kinds of less visible panopticons, for example in the context of social media. And Foucault already wrote about what is now called governance on the basis of data science. Panopticism is also about administration and data, leading to what Foucault calls "integral surveillance": methods first used locally but then – in the 18th and 19th century – by the state, for example by the police and the Napoleonic administration:

> People learned how to establish dossiers, systems of marking and classifying, the integrated accountancy of individual records. [...] But the permanent surveillance of a group of pupils or patients was a different matter. And, at a certain moment in time, these methods began to become generalised. (Foucault 1980, 71)

Today, we experience a further generalization of such methods, powered by AI. Current governance by data, or "algorithmic governance" (Sætra 2020, 4), leads to what Foucault (1977) called a "disciplinary society" that works analogously to Bentham's design for the panopticon, but now pervading all aspects of social life: the effects of disciplinary power are "not exercised from a single vantage point, but are mobile, multivalent and internal to the very fabric of our everyday life" (Downing 2008, 83). AI and data science can do this, for example, via social media and smartphones, which pervade the social life of people. As already explained, this raises concerns about freedom as autonomy, democracy, and capitalism. But with Foucault we can understand it also in terms of decentralized, smaller operations of power. For example, when using social media, people are not just the passive victims of authorities and corporations; other individual users also exercise forms of power by the way they interact with each other and with the platform. There are different forms of peer-to-peer surveillance and what Albrechtslund (2008) calls "self-surveillance" and "participatory" surveillance, which do not necessarily violate the user (unlike bullying) but can be playful and even empowering as they enable users to construct their identity, socialize with strangers, maintain friendships, and see opportunities for action. This approach reflects a decentralized, horizontal understanding of power, which could also be used to understand AI in terms of its micro-mechanisms of power.

That being said, centralist and hierarchical forms of power still exist. For example, AI can be used to support "state of emergency" versions of governmentality that, for example in response to terrorism, "decide on who will be detained, and who will not, who may see life outside the prison again and who may not" (Butler 2004, 62). In the name of security or actions against terror, AI may be part of forms of "algorithmic governmentality" (see again Rouvroy 2013) that are used to exercise state power in a way that delegates decisions about who is inside and outside the political community. Even liberal democracies in the EU increasingly use AI for border control. In the 21st century, forms of governmentality that readers of Foucault thought belonged to the past are back, now mediated and enabled by AI and data science. To fight the COVID-19 pandemic, police surveillance and traditional disciplining measures such as isolation and quarantine are used, but now enabled by high tech: AI helps with diagnosis via medical imaging technologies and developing medicines and vaccines, but also with contact tracing of individuals, forecasting the spread of the virus based on available data, and tracking and monitoring patients under home quarantine via smartphones or smart bracelets. In other words: AI helps with surveillance, and in a very vertical, top-down form. The "only" thing that was needed for this to happen was a pandemic. AI is a new biopolitical tool which enables new forms of surveillance and even new biopolitics of killing and letting die, with drones and triage systems (Rivero 2020). Yet following Foucault, we must stress that today most surveillance is not about political authorities (Big Brother), but happens outside formal political institutions, throughout the whole of society: today, AI can "see" everything and even "smell" everything, so-called "odorveillance" (Rieger 2019, 145).

If this is true, who gains new power, in addition to the state? If power emanates from new and different centers, who or what are they? One answer is: corporations, especially big tech. Véliz (2020) argues that by collecting our data, big tech companies and political actors transform knowledge into power. There is an asymmetry of power, since "they know almost everything about us" (86). AI enables surveillance and manipulation, but the data collection itself is already problematic. Véliz distinguishes between the hard and soft power of tech. The hard power is that data are taken even if we resist, for example refusing permission (55). Soft power, by contrast, works in a different, often manipulative, way: "[I]t makes us do something for the benefit of others under the pretence that it is for our own benefit. It recruits our will against ourselves. Under the influence of soft power, we engage in behaviour that undermines our best interests" (58–9). Véliz gives the example of scrolling down our Facebook newsfeed: we are hooked because we fear that we are missing out, and this is done on purpose: our attention is captured against our best interests (59). This is done as we use computers and smartphones, but devices such as personal robots and digital assistants are also used to exercise this soft power.

Knowledge, power, and the making and shaping of subjects and selves

Second, AI and data science are not only power-full tools in the sense that they enable discipline and surveillance. They also generate new knowledge and co-define who and what we are. Throughout his work after *Discipline and Punish*, Foucault argued not only that knowledge is an instrument of power but also that power produces knowledge and new subjects. Google becomes empowered by our data, but there is more: "[T]hat power allows Google to decide what counts as knowledge about you through its use of your personal data" (Véliz 2020, 51–2). The tech companies thus do not only act upon us but also construct us as human subjects. They produce our desires (e.g., the desire for scrolling) and make us into different beings with a different way of being in the world (Véliz 2020, 52). And even in the humanities these technologies are used, which also leads to new forms of knowledge and power. Through algorithmic discourse analysis, for example, knowledge is created in a non-anthropogenic way, bypassing human intentions and theories:

Data mining and text mining make patterns and thus forms of knowledge visible that are not necessarily exhausted in intentional questions. Here, everything that human intelligence, in its scientific narcissism, regards as its genuine field of activity – ordering and classifying things, identifying similarities, and creating genealogies – is relegated to algorithms. (Rieger 2019, 144)

According to Foucault (1980), individual identity is also the product of power: "The individual, with his identity and characteristics, is the product of a relation of power exercised over bodies, multiplicities, movements, desires, forces" (74). This identity production happens today in the more "horizontal" social structures and processes of social media, where we are under surveillance and disciplined not only by hierarchical agents of power such as governments and companies, but also by our peers and, in the end, by ourselves. Without being aware of it, we are working on our bodies and shape our self and identity. As we interact with others on social media and are analyzed and categorized by AI, we are not only the victims of capitalist governmentality and bio-power but also self-discipline, self-quantify, and self-produce our subjectivity. For Foucault, disciplined bodies are found everywhere in society; digital media and AI are fully part of that society.

This emphasis on bodies, which is continued, for instance, in feminist work by Butler, renders Foucault's approach to disciplining and the making of subjects very concrete, yet always connected to the societal level. Foucault (1980, 58) argued that different societies need different kinds of bodies: from the 18th century to the mid-20th century, disciplinary regimes in schools, hospitals, factories, families, and so on, involved heavy investment of the body with power, whereas afterwards more subtle forms of power were exercised over the body. Today, we can ask what kind of bodies are needed and created through disciplining by AI and other digital technologies, and what new subtle and less subtle forms of power these technologies enable. It seems that contemporary "AI society" needs bodies that can be *datafied*, quantified, and (im)mobilized to deliver these data and numbers via interaction with smartphones and other devices. This constitutes a much softer and less visible, but no less pervasive, form of power over our bodies. What AI does to us in terms of disciplining, power, and subjectivity is thus not a matter of merely "mental" operations or cognition, if "cognition" is understood as disembodied and entirely immaterial; it also has bodily effects. But taking into account the lessons of contemporary cognitive science (e.g., Varela, Thompson, and Rosch 1991), any cognition worth talking about is embodied cognition. Our thinking and experience depend on our body; the body plays an active role in cognitive processes. Moreover, if we take on board insights from posthumanism (e.g., Haraway – see the next chapter), the body is not just the biological body: it can also be understood as itself linked and merged with the material, as having a "cyborg" character. In this sense, the claim, made by some Marxian scholars, that immaterial labor is done is misleading: what we do with our bodies and minds is very much connected with the material technologies we use and has very physical consequences, including effects on our bodies, health, and well-being. For example, as we self-discipline, are disciplined, and produce our self and subjectivity through the use of AI-powered smartphones and their apps, this has effects on our muscles, eyes, and so on, and can lead to stress, negative emotions, sleep disorders, depression, and addiction. AI in this case might well be "virtual" or "immaterial" in the sense that it comes in the form of software and databases, but its use and effects are material and physical, involving body and mind. To use Marx's vampire metaphor: surveillance capitalism *sucks that living labor*.

However, power and the production of subjects, bodies, and knowledge is not necessarily a bad thing by itself, and in any case not necessarily violent or constraining. Foucault argued that power and force can also be exercised in subtle ways that are physical but not necessarily violent (Hoffmann 2014, 58). All depends on how it is done and what the results are. What does power produce and what forces does technology create?

Let me elaborate on Foucault's productive approach to power. The idea of the power-full and technological shaping of the self can also be based on the later work of Foucault, in which he writes about transformations of the self in ancient Greece and Christianity, which are achieved by applying "technologies of the self": one of the ways human beings develop knowledge about themselves. Technologies of the self

> permit individuals to affect by their own means or with the help of others a certain number of operations on their own bodies and souls,

thoughts, conduct, and way of being, so as to transform themselves in order to attain a certain state of happiness, purity, wisdom, perfection, or immortality. (Foucault 1988, 18)

Foucault does not see these "technologies" as material and distinguishes them from technologies of production. He is interested in the "hermeneutics of the self" and the virtue and practice of self-care in Greco-Roman philosophy and in Christian spirituality and practices (19). Revising Foucault in the light of contemporary philosophy of technology, however, one could see writing as a material technology of the self that helps self-care, self-constitution, and indeed the achievement of virtue. When ancient philosophers, Christian monks, and humanist scholars wrote about themselves, they exercised both care and power over themselves. One could then argue that technologies such as AI, which permit self-surveillance, self-tracking, self-care, and self-disciplining, are also used as "technologies of the self": not just for domination and disciplining by others – although this might still be the case, consider again the Marxian analysis and the earlier Foucault – but also for exercising a form of *power over oneself*. Consider health apps for disciplining eating and physical exercise or apps for meditation: they are used for self-care, but at the same time this involves an exercise of power over one's self, soul, and body, which leads to a specific kind of self-knowledge (e.g., quantification of the self), involves the operation of physical forces, and constitutes a particular kind of subject and body. Instead of constraining something pre-existing, power here is productive as it brings something (a self, a subject, a body) into being. In this sense, it is enabling rather than constraining. AI can be used within such practices of self-constitution. Critical questions should then be asked not only about what kind of self and subject AI produces, but also about what kind of self-care and practice of the self is involved. Technology itself does not have this power; it is the technology as used within a practice of self-care, self-disciplining, and so on. But the technology influences the particular kind of self-shaping. For example, one could claim that AI and data science produce a "quantified self" through a practice of self-tracking, which also produces a particular kind of knowledge: one that takes the form of numbers.

This making of the self can be further theorized by using the work of Judith Butler. Like Foucault, Butler sees power as productive, but for her this takes the form of the *performative* constitution of the self. Drawing on Austin's (1962) description of how some speech acts do things, she argues that our selves and identities – for example gender identities – are not essences but are performatively constituted (Butler 1988); gender is a kind of performance (Butler 1999). This renders these selves and identities neither fixed nor assumed (Loizidou 2007, 37). In line with Foucault, she thus argues that there is not only subjection (e.g., as disciplining) but also becoming a subject (e.g., subjectivation). But by stressing the performative dimension of this practice and operation, she claims that she renders her account of power less passive than Foucault's (Butler 1989). Power is about acts that constitute the subject. It is not just others who make us into something; we also shape ourselves, for example by saying things. And this is also a temporal matter: Butler (1993) understands performativity not as one act but as reiterative practice: "[P]erformativity must be understood not as a singular or deliberate 'act,' but, rather, as the reiterative and citational practice by which discourse produces the effects it names" (2). This could be reconciled with Foucault, who talks about practices of self-care. And inspired by Bourdieu (1990), one could add: self-constitution is a matter of *habitus*. Constitution of the self operates via the habitual and performative operation of forces upon oneself.

Yet Butler's conception of performativity and her conception of politics (Butler 1997) remain focused on language. Like in Foucault, the emphasis is on discourse. To this we must add the idea that self, identity, and gender are produced and performed not only through language but also through technological practices. Alongside writing, there are also other technological practices: Web 2.0 technologies (Bakardjieva and Gaden 2011) such as social media, but also AI. The constitution of the self through AI may well have linguistic aspects, but, as said, it is also deeply technological and material, such as when a "quantified self" is produced. Moreover, it is also always a social matter. Both self and other are shaped in the process. For example, through the use of running apps and other wearable self-tracking technologies, the other becomes an object of examination and competition (Gabriels and Coeckelbergh 2019).

These technological ways of self-shaping and self-care raise at least two problems. First, the quantification of self and other misleadingly suggests that the self or other can be reduced to a collection of digital information – that is, that the digital self is the actual self (see again datafication) – or, at least as problematic, that the digital self or other is *more* self than the non-digital self or other. The latter assumption seems operative in at least one transhumanist fantasy about immortality and resurrection through uploading. Kurzweil has imagined that machine learning will be able to reconstruct a digital version of his dead father, rendering it possible to talk to an avatar of him: "It will be so realistic it will be like talking to my father," indeed "it would be more like my father than my father would be, were he to live" (Berman 2011). Criticizing this, Andrejevic (2020) has argued that Kurzweil aims to create an idealized image of the self (and other) and one that is more coherent and consistent than an actual subject. But an actual subject is always "constituted by its gaps and inconsistencies" and hence any attempt at perfection of self and subject "amounts to an attempt to obliterate it" (1). Automation of mental production and the relevant human intelligence needed for it, too, tries to reconfigure and thereby obliterate the subject: by abstracting tasks away from motivations, intentions, and desires, "the reflexive layer of subjectivity" is sidestepped (5). This implies not only that human judgment and thinking are bypassed, as Arendt would agree, but also that the human subject is superfluous, if not annoyingly in the way. Just as the fantasy of an automated subject is challenged by the reality of actual subjects who "can be unpredictable, recalcitrant, and otherwise irrational in ways that threaten systems of control, management, and governance" (2), and hinder the smooth and frictionless running of automated society, the fantasy of the uploaded self tries to create a digital avatar that would be *no longer like a self or subject at all*. This is also a problem when we try to shape ourselves and others with the help of social media and AI: we try to shape ourselves and others into *somethings*, avatars perhaps, but no longer persons, selves, or subjects. Moreover, as Couldry and Mejias (2019, 171) point out by drawing on Hegel, being mediated is itself not a problem, but a life in which the reflective relation to oneself is missing, with no space to be with oneself, is not a free life.

Furthermore, all this self-shaping is tiring and potentially exploitative – and self-exploitation is also problematic. We have moved from Foucault's disciplinary society to what Han (2015) calls the "achievement society" (8). In chapter 3, we already saw that capitalism produces anxious selves who have internalized the imperative to perform and are afraid of being replaced by machines. Han argues that in contemporary society, prohibitions and commandments are replaced by "projects, initiatives, and motivation" (9). Whereas the disciplinary society produces lunatics and criminals, "achievement society creates depressives and losers" (9). Depressive individuals are tired of having to become themselves. Individuals exploit themselves, especially in work contexts in which they have to achieve and perform. They become machines. But it appears that resistance is impossible here since exploiter and exploited are the same: "Excess work and performance escalate into auto-exploitation" (11). Depression "erupts at the moment when the achievement-subject is *no longer able to be able [nicht mehr können kann]*" (10; Han's emphasis and German). This could be linked to a Marxian analysis: the capitalist system demands this self-exploitation. From the point of view of the capitalist, it is a brilliant system, since it seems that people have only themselves to blame when they do not sufficiently perform and achieve and when they fail to sufficiently work on themselves. Even in the private sphere, we constantly feel like we have to do this self-work. AI and related technologies are used to increase our work performance, but we also use them to work on ourselves, until we *cannot any longer [nicht mehr können]*. Even self-constitution has become a matter of achievement, promoted by technologies that monitor, analyze, and boost our performance until we can no longer perform and are burned out. To resist such a system of power and governmentality is difficult, since it seems that we only have ourselves to blame for not keeping up; we should have used the right kind of apps and have done more self-work. If we are depressed or burned out, it's our own fault, and a failure to achieve.

In principle, however, different self-shadings and different technologies of the self are possible. Foucault's theoretical framework leaves open the possibility that the productive, knowledge- and self-constituting use of power can also take other, empowering forms. Or to put it in terms of performance: different performances of the self are possible. Let me offer suggestions from my own work on performance and technology in order to show the possibilities of a performance-oriented view of power for understanding and evaluating AI.

Technoperformances, power, and AI

As we have seen, Butler uses the term "performance" to conceptualize the constitution of the self. But we can also use it to conceptualize technology use, highlight the way technology has power over us, and reveal connections between individual performances and their political context (Coeckelbergh 2019b; 2019c). Here the point of connecting technology with performance is not just to say that digital technology is used in art performances (Dixon 2007), but rather that performance can be used as metaphor and concept to think about technology. With regard to power, this approach enables us to describe and evaluate what happens in terms of power when technologies get more agency: I have argued that they *direct* and *choreograph* us (Coeckelbergh 2019b). As we engage in "technoperformances" (Coeckelbergh 2019c), technology increasingly takes a leading and organizing role. There is a sense in which we do not only perform with technology; "technology also performs with us." Humans are not absent; we co-perform and co-direct, co-choreograph. But the technology also shapes the performance. The question then is which plays, choreographies, and so on, we want to create with the technology and what our role is in these performances (Coeckelbergh 2019b, 155). Based on this approach, one could insist again that AI is not just an instrument used by humans to exercise power, but also has unintended effects, and that one of these effects can be described as follows: as and insofar as AI is given more agency, for example in the form of self-driving cars, robots, and algorithms that operate on the internet, but also as AI's unintended influence becomes more pervasive, it becomes a choreographer, director, and so on, of our movements, speech, emotions, and social life. It is not just a tool or a thing but organizes the way we do things. Again, this does not mean that humans are not involved or not accountable, but rather that AI has a more-than-instrumental role in that it shapes what we do and how we do things. It has the power to organize our performances and changes the field of forces and power-full relations.

Using the term "performance" in relation to AI also brings in a number of dimensions of technology use that relate to power. First, it enables us to say that the use of AI is always a social affair, understood as co-performance. It involves humans who interact and operate in a social context, and hence also a political context. It may also involve an "audience" which responds to its use. One could say that AI is always situated in this social environment, which, as Foucault shows, is pervaded by power. For example, use of AI by big tech takes place within a socio-political context and has an audience of users and citizens, who respond to what these companies do. This "audience" also has power and is part of the power relation. Second, if the use of AI is conceptualized as performance, this also means that the body is involved. As noted earlier, the fact that AI comes in an "immaterial" or "virtual" form, for example software, does not mean that there is no power effect on bodies. Technoperformances, like all performances, involve human bodies. This is in line with Foucault's and Butler's attention to the body, but does not exclusively attach the concept of body to discourse, knowledge, and identity. The way power works here is also quite literally about *movement*, moving bodies. When I use AI via an app on my smartphone, I am not a disembodied user using only "mental" or "cognitive" functions: I am moving my body and hands, my body is partly immobilized, and so on. This is so because AI and its designers choreograph the movements that are necessary to operate the device and app in a certain way, and thereby exercise power over me and my body. Third, the notion of performance also brings in the temporal aspect. The exercise of technopower by and through AI takes place in time and even configures time, in the sense that it shapes our experience of time and configures our stories, days, and lives. For example, we regularly pick up our phone and look at messages and recommendations; this becomes part of our daily routine. In this sense, AI has the power to define my time. And by means of data collection and data analysis, my story is configured in terms of the statistical categories and profiles made by AI. This happens not only at the individual level but also at the cultural and societal level: our time becomes the time of AI and AI shapes the narrative of our societies.

This approach resonates with Foucauldian thinking, including Foucauldian dance and performance theory. Kozel (2007) has referred to power and knowledge in order to make claims about what McKenzie (2001, 19) calls "the mechanisms of performative power." Performance is seen as "distributed across temporalities, networks, and bodies of all sorts" (Kozel 2007, 70). And so, one could add, is power: the power in and of technoperformances is also distributed across temporalities, networks, and bodies. Moreover, we also meet again a "productive" view of power: AI has the power to shape our time (in a particular way). In line with Foucault and with Butler (1988), one could argue that technoperformances that involve AI do not only discipline us and put us under surveillance, but also constitute us as new subjects, citizens, and identities. They also produce a particular kind of self and subjectivity. I come to understand myself in a particular way through the use of AI. This can be understood in narrative terms or otherwise. For example, through these technoperformances, we may get a networked sense of self (Papacharissi 2011) or, as I suggested earlier, a datafied sense of self. Cheney-Lippold (2017) argues that algorithms and the corporations that employ them, such as Google and Facebook, use data to construct our worlds and identities. In this sense, and as Cheney-Lippold's title says, "we are data," and we increasingly believe it. From a critical theory perspective, it should be pointed out that this is incredibly useful to companies whose business model it is to monetize our data, such as Facebook. We are not only consumers but also at the same time producers of data: we work for these companies, who exploit us by means of what Fuchs and coauthors (2012, 57) call "a panoptic sorting machine," which identifies the interests of users, classifies them, and then enables targeted advertisements. But I add that this construction of world and self – and the exploitation related to it – is not just something that happens to us. Our technoperformances with AI develop as we engage with the technology; it is an active process and is the result of human effort. It is not just that others or AI algorithms make us into data. Through our performances with the technology, *we also make ourselves into data* as we technoperformatively constitute our selves on social media and elsewhere. We thus contribute to both our self-constitution and our exploitation.

Seeing technology in terms of (techno)performances is in line with conceptions of technology that see it as activity. Such conceptions enable us to bring in the social and political dimension (Lyon 1994). Technology can be about artifacts and things, for sure, but in order to study its political dimension, we need to look at what we do with technology and what technology does to us, and how both are embedded in a social (and knowledge) context. Seeing technology as activity and performance also enables us to stress again that humans are always involved. While contemporary directions in philosophy of technology such as postphenomenology rightly proclaim that technologies "do" things (Verbeek 2005), in the sense that they co-shape human perception and action (e.g., a microwave shapes our eating habits, ultrasound technology shapes how we experience pregnancy, etc.), the doings of technology also always involve humans. I will return to this point when I consider posthumanist views in the next chapter.

Finally, given that humans continue to co-direct and co-shape their social, bodily, and temporal performances, and thus participate in the exercise and circulation of power, we must ask *which* humans (co-)choreograph our technoperformances, and if the participation in these performances is always voluntary. As Parviainen (2010) asks: who is choreographing us? For example, one could claim that big tech choreographs us by means of AI embedded in our apps and devices, and increasingly designs what we do and shapes our stories, but that since we are usually not aware of this and since the technologies are designed to be persuasive, our participation in these performances and stories can hardly count as voluntary. And if technoperformances are always linked to a wider social and political context, it is important to ask who is *allowed* to participate in the performances of AI (in both use and development), that is, who is included and who is excluded, and what the conditions of this participation are.

First, many of us are not only given a pseudo choice (Bietti 2020) when it comes to consent to usage but are also excluded when it comes to shaping the development of AI and how it is used. We are in the hands of big tech for this. Even governments often just go with what the tech sector offers; in many countries, regulation is minimal. A performance-oriented perspective enables us to ask critical questions about this: who are the actors and choreographers in the performance? Who is excluded from acting and choreographing? Which actors and choreographers have more power than others? And can we develop strategies to escape full control? These questions relate again to the discussion about democracy.

Second, AI performances can also be highly political in the sense of being linked to governmental politics. Using the choreography concept, Parviainen and I have argued that AI and robotics are used in the context of political interest and strategies (Parviainen and Coeckelbergh 2020). We show that performances with Sophia, a humanoid robot that is claimed to involve AI, are linked to AI politics: "The performances with Sophia did not only serve the interest of one private company (Hanson Robotics); they also served the interests of those who seek to expand the technologies involved and the relevant markets connected to these technologies" (7). Using the term "power," one could also frame this as follows: the private sector involved in the development of AI and robotics stages technoperformances as a way to expand markets and hence increase their power and profit. Similarly, governments may support such performances and participate in them in order to realize their plans and strategies with regard to AI, thus increasing *their* power in response to competitors, that is, other nations. Furthermore, discussions about the intelligence or ethical standing of social robots may distract from this political dimension, since they make it seem as if only technical or ethical questions can be asked about AI and robots: questions concerning the immediate interaction and environment of the technology but not the broader societal and political field. This misleadingly suggests that these technologies are power neutral and politically neutral. Performances with AI and the related discussions may thus hide that, like all technologies, AI is and can be very political and power-full. Researchers and journalists can reveal this wider political context, thus linking local and concrete AI performances to what happens at the "macro" level of politics and its power games.

This use of the term "performance" and its relations to power thus offers a framework for taking a critical perspective on AI, which is compatible with, and can be supported by, both Marxian analyses and Foucauldian approaches. It helps to reveal the myriad ways in which AI is connected to power: power being exercised in and through technoperformances and power circulating between these performances and a wider field of power and power players such as corporations and governments.

Conclusion and remaining questions

This chapter has shown how talking about power and AI enables us to bring in social and political theory that helps to conceptualize the political aspects of AI. Naturally, this exercise was not only about power but also linked to other political concepts and issues. For example, the discussion about nudging relates to problems regarding freedom, and the issue of bias already figured in chapter 3 on equality and justice. More could be said about any of these links. For example, the issue of bias in AI (Bozdag 2013; Criado Perez 2019; Granka 2010) can be framed as a power issue, as well as being about justice and equality: if there is bias in the algorithmic filtering, search algorithms, and data sets on which AI is trained, then this has to do with people exercising power over others. One could also say that there is a particular power structure in place (e.g., capitalist, patriarchal, etc.) in a particular society, which leads to bias through the use of AI. It seems that a plurality of concepts is useful to unpack this. Nevertheless, the concept of power has been a helpful lens through which we could analyze and discuss the politics of AI. The chapter offers yet another, unique way to conceptualize that technology is political and *how* it is political. It shows how talking about power helps us to analyze what exactly is happening and what could be problematic with it.

This conceptual bringing together of technology and politics, and especially the claim that AI has non-instrumental effects on power, remains problematic from a modern point of view, since in modernity technology and politics find themselves in separate domains. The first is supposed to be about technical and material things, whereas politics is supposed to be about humans and society. This modern idea has roots in ancient philosophy, at least since Aristotle, and continues to exert its influence today: AI is assumed to be politically neutral, and politics is assumed to be about the ends for which humans use AI. The discussions in this chapter cross this modern divide, for example when talking about how AI shapes our self, creates new forms of subjectivity, and choreographs us. In power-full AI performances, means and ends mix, and in the end so also do humans and technology. However, as stressed repeatedly, the idea is not that humans are replaced by technology or that technology is doing all this on its own. The point of applying terms such as choreography to AI was not that humans are not involved in exercises of power and technoperformances, but rather that AI is sometimes given more agency and, through its unintended effects, co-shapes how we do things and who/what we are. In this sense, AI has power over us.

Blurring the line between technology and politics, in particular between AI and power, we can thus speak of AI as "artificial power": not because AI is *all*-powerful, but because power is exercised through AI. AI is only power-full and political as part of human technoperformances that shape what we do and who/what we are.

Yet there is another, related boundary that deserves discussion: the human/non-human boundary. It is often assumed that politics, and hence also the politics of AI, is all about humans. But this can and has been contested. This is the topic of the next chapter.

6

What about Non-Humans? Environmental Politics and Posthumanism

Introduction: Beyond a human-centered politics of AI and robotics

Most theories discussed in the previous chapters assume that political philosophy, and therefore also applying political philosophy to AI, is about politics for humans. Political principles like freedom, justice, equality, and democracy are supposed to be about freedom for humans, justice for humans, and so on. The *demos*, the public, and the body politic are assumed to consist of humans and their institutions. And most people believe that the term "power" is only applicable to human–human relations. If power circulates through the social body, as Foucault argues, then this body is conceived of as exclusively consisting of humans. Moreover, the ethics and politics of AI and robotics is often framed in an anthropocentric way: it is claimed that AI and robotics should be human-centered, as opposed to being driven by technology and economics. But what happens if we challenge these assumptions, and open up the boundaries of the political to non-humans? What does this mean for the politics of AI and robotics, and how can political philosophy and related theory help us to conceptualize this?

This chapter addresses these questions by first considering political theory that already crossed the human/non-human boundary: theory concerning animals and the natural environment. I pay special attention to relatively recent arguments about the political status of animals, in particular those anchored in relational and posthumanist approaches. Then the chapter discusses what this shift in political theory implies for the politics of AI and robotics. It asks two types of questions. First, it considers the impact AI has on non-humans (e.g., animals) and the environment. Should political thinking about AI and robots consider the consequences for non-humans such as (non-human) animals and ecosystems, given that the latter may have political status? If so, what concepts can be used to justify this? Second, can AI systems and robots themselves have political status? Can they be a kind of citizens, for example? How do transhumanism and posthumanism bear upon this question? For example, could and should AI take over political control, and how can we reimagine the political and the social in a way that includes non-humans?

Not only humans count, politically: The political status of animals and (non-human) nature

In animal ethics and environmental philosophy, we find proposals to extend the boundaries of moral and political consideration to non-human animals and the environment. Given the topic of this book, I will focus on *political* consideration and in addition I will limit the scope of my discussion to some of the main arguments about the political status of *animals*, although I will also touch upon environmental politics and the politics of climate change.

A well-known work in this area is Singer's *Animal Liberation* (2009), which famously offers a utilitarian argument for the liberation of animals we use and kill for the production of food, clothes, and other purposes: we should evaluate the consequences of these practices for the animals, and if we cause their suffering, we should reduce that suffering and, if necessary, abolish the practices altogether. But while Singer framed this as an ethics, the book can easily be read as a political-philosophical work, appealing to key political principles. For a start, it is aimed at liberation and has been used as a justification to liberate animals by the animal liberation movement. The preface to the first edition of the book in 1975 starts with the words: "This book is about the tyranny of human over nonhuman animals" (8). Singer thus formulates his ethics by using a political term: tyranny, the opposite of political freedom. But he does not only appeal to political freedom. He also talks about considering the interests of animals, extending equality principles from humans to non-human animals, and ending prejudice and discrimination, which have a long history. His central argument concerning speciesism relies on an accusation of a particular kind of bias and discrimination. The goal to liberate animals from abuse and killing in all domains is justified by the argument that, just like humans, most animals feel pain, and that therefore treating them like this is "speciesism": the unjust discrimination of non-human animals based on the sole fact that they belong to a different species. It is "a prejudice or attitude of bias in favour of the interests of members of one's own species and against those of members of other species" (6). And because most of us (as meat eaters) are the oppressors and discriminators, change is difficult. He compares the animal liberation movement to other important political movements: the civil rights movement, whereby black people only got rights because they demanded them (whereas animals cannot speak for themselves); the struggle for the abolition of slavery; and the feminist movement with its protests against sexism. This supports his claim that protest and struggle are necessary to change things. Singer's book is thus as much about ethics as it is about political philosophy. His utilitarian ethics, which is usually what philosophers focus on when responding to his work, is in fact linked to a set of political-philosophical concepts that nearly span the full range I covered in the previous chapters. Note also that Singer takes a universalist position in his ethics and political philosophy: he does not use identity as a criterion, but argues on the basis of the universal capacity for suffering, regardless of the species.

Other arguments for giving animals political considerations, which also stay within the universalist liberal tradition, rely on the political principle of justice. For example, one can make a contractarian argument about justice for animals. An influential theory in this area is Rawls's theory of justice. Rawls excludes animals from his theory of justice (Garner 2003), and this kind of contractarianism generally rests on the importance of human rationality. This is why Nussbaum (2006) chooses to rely on the concept of capabilities when it comes to giving animals moral and political standing in terms of justice: like humans, animals are also entitled to capabilities to function and flourish. They may not possess human rationality, but they have their own species-specific abilities and we should respect their own dignity. Nussbaum considers what her list of capabilities/entitlements mean for animals. For example, animals are entitled to a healthy life, which implies that we need laws that forbid cruel treatment (394). This is by itself an interesting application of political theory: initially meant for humans, it is then applied to animals. (Note also that there is an interesting link between Nussbaum's capability approach and ancient virtue ethics and politics focused on human flourishing; however, I will not further discuss this here.)

However, some authors have nevertheless proposed that justice for animals could be argued for on a contractarian basis. One could modify the original Rawlsian position in such a way that the veil of ignorance includes ignorance about whether one will end up as a human or an animal. For instance, in Rowlands's (2009) version, rationality is hidden behind the veil of ignorance, since this is an undeserved natural advantage. Another route is to stress cooperation between humans and animals. I have argued that animals could be drawn into the sphere of distributive justice if they are part of a cooperative scheme (Coeckelbergh 2009b): the idea is that humans and non-humans are interdependent in various ways and that they sometimes cooperate. If and when this is the case (e.g., for domestic animals), then these animals should be considered as part of the sphere of justice. Also shifting the ethical debate to the realm of political theory, Donaldson and Kymlicka, in *Zoopolis* (2011), have argued in a similar vein that we have relational obligations towards animals and that we should include them in the cooperative project of shared citizenship. The authors admit that animals may have a reduced capacity for political agency, but they can nevertheless be considered as citizens.

This is also what I have called a "relational" view (Coeckelbergh 2012): instead of intrinsic properties or capabilities, Donaldson and Kymlicka emphasize human–animal relations. These relations give us duties, for example the duty to care for animals which are dependent upon us. This does not imply that all animals have the same form of citizenship. Like in human societies, the authors argue, some animals should be full members of our political communities (e.g., domesticated animals), whereas others will have their own communities (e.g., animals in the wild). However, Garner (2012) has criticized such arguments since, according to him, authors who argue that the original position should be redefined actually rely on a principle outside the contract, and the reliance on social cooperation works for domesticated animals but not for others. One could reply that (1) it is not clear why these contractarians should be held to higher standards than Rawls, who also refers to pre-existing normative judgments (in his case, for instance, the view that justice only applies to persons), and (2) that contractarian arguments are indeed limited when it comes to giving *political* consideration to animals, but that luckily there are other, moral arguments that have a wider scope of application, which can justify much wider protections but do not concern *political* rights and duties, strictly speaking. We could give moral consideration to many animals on the basis of all kinds of arguments (e.g., arguments based on sentience), but not all of these animals may qualify as beneficiaries of *political* justice. For example, one could argue that we *might* have moral duties towards, say, a wild animal that is suffering in the woods (e.g., on the basis of a duty to relieve suffering *à la* Singer and compassion), but this is not a *political* duty since the animal is not part of our political community.

In response to this restriction, one could call for broadening the scope of political community to all animals, although it is difficult to say what this means. For example, if we give political status to wild animals, what are our duties towards them and in what sense, exactly, are they part of our political communities? One could also go beyond animals and discuss if, say, rivers or ecosystems also should have political status, in addition to specific animals. For example, in 2018, Colombia's Supreme Court granted the Amazon forest personhood, and in New Zealand the Whanganui River and ecosystem have legal standing. The latter could be justified by relying on a moral argument concerning intrinsic value, but it could also be supported by a relational, political argument about the relation of interdependence between the river (e.g., spiritual characteristics) and the indigenous Iwi people (and of course both arguments could be connected). A similar debate can be held about the value of the earth or the planet as a whole. For example, in 2008, Ecuador moved to protect the rights of the Pachamama (nature) in its constitution, and in 2010, Bolivia – influenced by indigenous Andean worldviews which see the earth as a living being – passed the Law of the Rights of Mother Earth, which defines Mother Earth as "a collective subject of public interest" and enumerates several rights to which this entity is entitled, including life and the diversity of life (Vidal 2011). One could frame this as respecting the intrinsic value of Mother Earth or as respecting the political rights of the indigenous people, or both.

In environmental ethics, there is a long-standing discussion about anthropocentrism (e.g., Callicott 1989; Curry 2011; Næss 1989; Rolston 1988) and intrinsic value (Rønnow-Rasmussen and Zimmerman 2005). For example, whereas Regan (1983) restricts intrinsic value to higher animals, Callicott (1989), Rolston (1988), and Leopold (1949) argue for an ethic that attributes intrinsic value to species, habitats, ecosystems, and (in Rolston's case) the biosphere. This view goes against anthropocentric moral philosophy (which only recognizes the intrinsic value of humans) and is grounded in an ecological understanding of nature (McDonald 2003). While these discussions are framed in terms of ethics, they could be expanded to include political considerations based on intrinsic value, and be used to justify the rights of the wider natural entities mentioned above.

Posthumanist theory also offers a basis for a non-anthropocentric approach, and could be interpreted as lending support to giving non-human animals political consideration. *Posthumanism*, meaning either "after" or "beyond" humanism, refers to a number of theoretical directions that are critical of humanism and of contemporary society and culture. It is to be distinguished from *transhumanism*, which is about enhancement of human capacities and – in at least one variant – sees AI as replacing humans or taking over power from humans (see later in this chapter). In its philosophical form, posthumanism deconstructs "the human" and hierarchical and dualist perspectives (Ferrando 2019), and is hence against anthropocentrism. Since it questions the privileged position of the human in the Western philosophical tradition and draws attention to non-humans and hybridization, it is post-anthropocentric, although it can certainly not be reduced to that position (Braidotti 2016, 14). For example, in some versions there is a strong emphasis on structural discrimination and injustice. Consider feminist posthumanism and post-colonial theory. One should also acknowledge that there is variety in the Western tradition with regard to anthropocentrism (e.g., compare Kant and Hegel with Aristotle and Marx): there are degrees of anthropocentrism (Roden 2015, 11–12). Posthumanism's post-anthropocentrism and anti-dualism are linked: in addition to dualisms such as subject/object and male/female, it seeks to overcome the dualisms human/non-human, human/animal, animate/inanimate, and so on. Therefore, it also tries to defuse the Western fear of technology: instead of seeing technologies as instrumental or threatening, it stresses what Derrida (1976; 1981) and Stiegler (1998), among others, call humans' "originary technicity" (see also Bradley 2011; MacKenzie 2002, 3) and creates imaginaries of living together with machine others. Posthumanism proposes more open ontologies that include technology. AI is then no longer seen as a threat to human autonomy; after its work of deconstruction, there is no longer a "the human" and its non-relational autonomy that could be threatened. The subject is never fully in control and is always dependent on others. Congruent with feminist accounts of relational autonomy, both the human and the subject are seen as deeply relational. As Rouvroy (2013) has argued (following Butler and Althusser), there is no such thing as full autonomy. Moreover, posthumanism is a philosophical but also a political project. Alongside postcolonial, Foucauldian, and feminist approaches (among others), for example in the work of Haraway, Braidotti, and Hayles, it includes criticisms of the violence and totalizing inflicted on non-human animals by those holding a human-centered, human exceptionalist worldview and politics (Asdal, Druglitrø, and Hinchliffe 2017). It acknowledges, moreover, that we – humans and non-humans – are all interdependent and that we all depend on the earth (Braidotti 2020, 27). (And note that in philosophy of technology there are also other non-anthropocentric ethical frameworks that come from different theoretical directions, for example Floridi's [2013] information ethics.)

Let me unpack this set of posthumanist theories, with a view to first highlighting their different attitude towards animals and the natural environment. A key figure in posthumanism is Haraway. After her "political-fictional (political-scientific) analysis" in the "Cyborg Manifesto" (2000), which already crossed the natural–artificial boundary with the figure of the cyborg ("creatures simultaneously animal and machine"),

Haraway argues for a politics committed to the flourishing of animals in at least two ways. First, she claims that there are "companion species" (Haraway 2003), such as dogs, and that our relations, living together, and in the end co-evolution with such non-human significant others lead to co-constitution of each other's identities. On the basis of this view, one could argue for giving moral and political status to at least those animals that count as companion species. Second, Haraway further opens up the boundaries of the political to animals with her concepts of *making kin* and *multispecies* politics. Responding to the discussion about the Anthropocene, which highlights the agency of humans when it comes to shaping the earth, she argues that not only humans have transformed the earth but also other "terraformers," such as bacteria, and that there are many interactions between biological species and technologies. Haraway (2015) thinks that politics should promote the "flourishing for rich multispecies assemblages that include people" but also the "more-than-human" and "other-than-human" (160). Based on this "compostist" (161) view, the body politic is expanded to all kinds of entities, with which we can make kin and to whom/which we have to respond. As Haraway puts it in *Staying with the Trouble* (2016): we are responsible "for shaping conditions for multispecies flourishing" (29), and this responding forms bonds that create new kinds of kinship. Yet in a footnote she warns about generalization and stresses respect for diversity and historical situations, making a direct link to human politics (in particular US politics):

Making kin must be done with respect for historically situated, diverse kinships that should not be either generalized or appropriated in the interest of a too-quick common humanity, multispecies collective, or similar category. [...] The sorry spectacle of many white liberals in the US, in the wake of African American and allied organizing against police murders of Black people and other outrages, resisting #BlackLivesMatter by insisting that #AllLivesMatter is instructive. Making alliances requires recognizing specificities, priorities, and urgencies. [...] Intending to make kin while not seeing both past and ongoing colonial and other policies for extermination and/or assimilation augurs for very dysfunctional "families," to say the least. (207)

Another posthumanist, Wolfe, explores the implications of Foucault's concept of biopower and biopolitics for "trans-species relations" (Wolfe 2010, 126). In *Before the Law: Humans and Other Animals in a Biopolitical Frame* (2013), he questions the exclusion of animals in the Western tradition from Aristotle to Heidegger. He criticizes Heidegger's assumption that humanity and animality are "ontologically opposed zones" (5–6) and uses the concept of biopolitics – inspired by Foucault (Wolfe 2017) – to argue that we are all animals before the law:

> The biopolitical point is no longer "human" vs. "animal"; the biopolitical point is a newly expanded community of the living and the concerns we should all have with where violence and immunitary protection fall within it, because we are all, after all, potentially animals before the law. (Wolfe 2013, 104–5)

Massumi (2014) also queries the exclusion of animals from the political. He questions the human–animal dichotomy in Western humanism and metaphysics and places humans on "the animal continuum" (3). Questioning the image we have of ourselves as standing apart from other animals, practices of exclusion and holding ourselves at a distance (e.g., in the zoo, the laboratory, or in front of a screen), and typological thinking itself with its category separations, he proposes an "integrally animal politics" instead of "a human politics of the animal" (2). The focus is on animal play and on "becoming-animal" (56–7): a term that is influenced by Deleuze and Guattari (1987) and process philosophy, and which is meant to reject hierarchical and rigid thinking about humans and animals and to problematize the oppression of non-human animals.

Similarly, Braidotti (2017) argues for rethinking subjectivity "as a collective assemblage that encompasses human and nonhuman actors, technological mediation, animals, plants, and the planet as a whole" (9). And she adds a specific normative, *political* view: we need to work towards a more egalitarian relationship to non-human others (10) and reject "the dominant configurations of the human as the king of creation" (15). She proposes zoe-centered egalitarianism, where "zoe" refers to the non-human, vital force of life (16). Influenced by Deleuze and Spinoza, she argues for a monistic approach and stresses compassionate acknowledgment of interdependence with non-anthropomorphic others (22). Cudworth and Hobden (2018) also see posthumanism as an emancipatory project: they aim to decenter the human but not lose the possibility of critical engagement with the crises of our time: ecological challenges and worldwide inequality (13). Their critical posthumanism explores alternatives to neoliberalism (16–17) and is "terraist" in the sense that it is "a politics for all that lives" (136). We are embedded in a relational landscape and share vulnerabilities with other creatures and living things. Influenced by Haraway, Cudworth and Hobden write about the precarity of vulnerable embodied "critters." (For work on vulnerability in digital times from a more existential point of view, see also Coeckelbergh 2013 and Lagerkvist 2019.) We are called to imagine a more inclusive future beyond neoliberalism, beyond the Anthropocene and Capitalocene, and (following Latour) beyond modernity (Cudworth and Hobden 2018, 137).

Latour (1993; 2004) is known for his non-modern view of science and society, which questions human/things and nature/culture distinctions when it comes to theorizing the social and the political. According to Latour, (the debate about) global warming is a hybrid, a mix of politics, science, technology, and nature. He argues for political ecology without the idea of nature. Inspired by Latour and Ingold, I have also questioned use of the term "nature" in several publications (e.g., Coeckelbergh 2015b; 2017). Moreover, as Alaimo (2016) has noted, the term "nature" "has long been enlisted to support racism, sexism, colonialism, homophobia, and essentialisms" (11) and is hence far from politically neutral. Posthumanists thus radically redraw the lines of the political community: not only humans but also non-humans (can) become part of it. This does not necessarily lead to the absence of lines or the absence of exclusion, but it does no longer accept the dogma that there is a deep gulf between humans and non-humans when it comes to politics. Posthuman theorists also question the very distinction between the ethical and the political. According to Alaimo, "even the smallest, most personal ethical practices in the domestic sphere are inextricably tied to any number of massive political and economic predicaments, such as global capitalism, labor and class injustice, climate injustice, neoliberalism, neocolonialism, industrial agriculture, factory farming, pollution, climate change, and extinction" (10–11). As such, posthumanists defend a less detached approach and agree with those environmental activists who argue that we should change our lives instead of making detached assertions about, for example, "nature." (Many environmentalists do, however, continue to refer to "nature," which is one reason why there is no full overlap between environmentalism and posthumanism.)

Some posthumanist theorists use Marx. For example, Atansoski and Vora (2019) think that Marx can still be "applied to techno-utopian fantasies of a postcapitalist, posthuman world" (96) and combine this with an approach focused on race, colonialism, and patriarchy. An interesting view that combines Marxism with an ecological approach is Moore's analysis of capitalism-in-nature, which questions the nature/society binary. He argues that to see nature as external is a condition of capital accumulation; instead, we should see capitalism as a way of organizing nature (Moore 2015). He criticizes those who speak of cyborgs, assemblages, networks, and hybrids for not escaping Cartesian binary thinking.

Related to posthumanism is also the interesting environmental politics concept of multispecies justice, which questions anthropocentric accounts of justice: it challenges human exceptionalism and the idea that humans are separate and separable from other species (Celermajer et al. 2021, 120). Tschakert (2020) highlights the non-human dimension of climate change and argues that the climate emergency demands that principles and practices of justice be revisited to encompass both the human and the natural world. She shows the interconnections between climate and multispecies justice by exploring encounters through which to recognize the non-human "Others" with which our lives are intertwined (3). In legal theory, there is also more thinking about who or what belongs to "communities of justice" (Ott 2020, 94), for example about the legal status of non-humans in the Anthropocene in relation to injustices within the earth system. Gellers (2020) proposes to widen communities of justice to include both natural and artifactual non-humans as legal subjects.

Now *if* (some?) animals and the natural environment have moral and political status, and if the political community is opened up to non-humans, then what does this mean for the politics of AI and robotics?

Implications for the politics of AI and robotics

If one leaves anthropocentrism behind and expands the political to animals and non-human nature, one could develop at least two kinds of positions regarding the potential implications for AI. First, one could claim that the use and development of AI should take into account that animals, the environment, and so on, have a moral and political status, and hence avoid harm to these natural entities and, if possible and preferably, positively contribute to more environmentally friendly practices and to solving problems such as climate change. One could promote environmentally and climate friendly AI. Second, one could claim that AI itself has a political status, and that hence we should talk about freedom, justice, democracy, political rights, and so on, *for AI*, or at least some kinds of AI – whatever that means. Let me unpack these positions and point to a number of theoretical resources available for their further development.

The political significance of the impact of AI on non-humans and natural environments

The first position is agnostic about the political status of AI itself (i.e., whether AI would count itself as a non-human that needs to be included in the political community), but claims that given the political value and interests of natural entities, the politics of AI can no longer be conceived of in an anthropocentric way. According to this position, AI should not be merely human-centered (i.e., oriented towards the value and interests of humans), let alone capital-centered, but should also be directed at the value and interests of natural entities such as animals, ecosystems, and the earth. The point here is not that animals can be studied – for example, some AI researchers take inspiration from biology for the design of robots or adopt its methods of social organization (Parikka 2010) – but that animals also have political value and interests on their own, which should be respected. When developing and using AI, then, one should take into account the consequences of the technology for animals, the natural environment, and the climate.

These consequences are not necessarily bad. AI also helps with tackling climate change and other environmental problems, for example when the use of machine learning to analyze data and run simulations enhances our scientific understanding of climate change and environmental problems, or when it helps to track illegal extraction of natural resources. And perhaps AI could also assist us in relating to animals, for example by helping with the management and conservation of habitats. But at the same time, the technology can also contribute to these problems in the first place. Sometimes this is very clear and visible. For example, AI-powered personal assistants in the home may hit pets or confuse them with their speech; AI used to organize agriculture and meat production may systematically lead to harm for animals; and AI used in industrial production may have detrimental effects on the climate and the environment. Yet even if all this is in principle visible to the eye of the user or observer, human-centered politics has a blind spot for such cases, since it is focused on politics for humans, and hence also on the politics of AI for humans. Opening up politics to non-humans helps us to reveal, imagine, and discuss these problems.

However, often use of AI has consequences that are more remote and less visible at the point of use. Here an important topic, which I already mentioned earlier but which deserves more attention, is the environmental and climate impact of AI in terms of energy use and use of resources. Computation required for some types of machine learning has increased dramatically, and this consumes a lot of energy, which is often not sourced from renewables. For example, the training of neural networks for natural language processing (NLP) requires considerable resources through their use of electricity and (hence) generates a sizable carbon footprint. Training a single NLP model can lead to emissions of carbon dioxide equivalent that are five times the amount produced by an average car over its lifetime (Strubell, Ganesh, and McCallum 2019). Currently researchers are trying to find ways to deal with this problem, for example training on less data or even reducing the number of bits needed to represent the data (Sun et al. 2020). Major IT companies such as Apple and Google have made renewable commitments. Nevertheless, most tech companies still rely on fossil fuels and as a whole the sector has a significant global carbon footprint. According to a Greenpeace report, in 2017, the energy footprint of the sector was already estimated at 7 percent of global electricity and is expected to rise (Cook et al. 2017; see also AI Institute 2019).

Use of streaming services – in combination with AI recommender systems – is part of the problem, since this requires
more data. The production of electronic devices that work
with AI also requires extraction of raw materials, which has
social and environmental consequences. Like historical forms of
colonialism, "data colonialism" (Couldry and Meijas 2019, xix)
goes hand in hand with the exploitation of natural resources:
the current exploitation of humans is not happening "instead
of natural resources" (xix) but in addition to, and based on,
extraction of natural resources. Therefore, the use of AI and
other digital technology does not necessarily lead to a demate-
rialization of the economy, as some hope. It also leads to more
consumption and hence more "ecological pressure" (Dauvergne
2020, 257). Similarly, surveillance capitalism is not just about
the destruction of human dignity but also has an environmental
side. The fact that these environmental and climate consequences
are not so visible at the point of use, but often happen in a place
remote from the particular use of AI, does not render them less
politically significant or less politically problematic. Moreover,
while, as mentioned, AI can help to fight climate change (Rolnick
et al. 2019), this does not necessarily compensate for the
problems indicated.

Based on this analysis, one could then argue, normatively,
that the impact of AI in terms of carbon footprint and environmental consequences is politically problematic for two reasons.
First, global warming/climate change and depletion of natural
resources have consequences for humans and human societies,
which are usually assumed to have a political status, and which
are dependent on the natural environment and the climate conditions. Second, based on the arguments regarding the political
interests, intrinsic value, and so on, of *non-humans*, one could
add that this is also problematic because of *their* political
status. If specific animals, ecosystems, and the earth as a whole
are impacted by AI – either directly through, for example, the
extraction of raw materials for AI devices or the AI-controlled
management of animals raised for food, or indirectly through the
destruction of habitats and the multifaceted impact of climate
change due to carbon-based electricity production, needed for
the operation of AI – then this impact is politically problematic
because the *animals*, *environments*, and so on, and not just
humans, count and should count politically.

Yet the idea of a shift to a non-anthropocentric politics of AI should not be classified away as being merely about one political value or principle such as "non-humans," "the climate," or "the environment"; instead, it resonates through all the principles and discussions we have visited and constructed in the previous chapters. For example, if (some) animals count politically, then we should also consider *their* freedom, talk about inter-species justice, ask if these animals could also be citizens in a democracy, and so on. Then the politics of AI is no longer human-centered but centered on interests and needs we share with some other animals, *and* specific interests and needs we do not share with them but still hold politically important. A non-anthropocentric turn to AI politics would not mean seeing animals, the environment, and climate as an extra consideration to an existing framework, but instead would constitute a fundamental change to the very idea of the political itself, which has been expanded to include non-humans and their interests.

Moreover, geopolitics – defined here as the politics of the earth or the planet – needs to be redefined once we remove humans from the center. From the perspective of a non-anthropocentric view and in tune with the posthumanist ideas mentioned above, it is no longer appropriate to talk about the "Anthropocene," since it may suggest that humans are central and in control, or *should* be central and in control. Instead, it is important to stress that we share the earth and the planet with many other beings. It may be that humans have assumed a hyper agency and treat the planet and its human and non-human inhabitants as their spaceship that can and must be managed and perhaps re-engineered, with the help of AI and other technologies. But this is the *problem*, not the solution. A non-anthropocentric politics of AI would be less technocentric, and problematize such an attitude and way of doing things: it would mean questioning AI as a solution to all our problems, and at least considering the idea of loosening our grip on the planet rather than increasing control by means of AI and data science. Once we question technosolutionism (Morozov 2013) or what Broussard (2019) calls "technochauvinism" – the belief that tech is always the solution – we no longer see AI as the magic solution to all our problems, and pay more attention to the limits of what it can do: for us and for non-humans.

Political status for AI itself?

The second position does not see AI as just an instrument in the service of humans or even non-humans, but also considers the possibility that some AI systems themselves gain political status, for example in the form of "machines" – whatever that means. The idea is that AI is not, or should not be, merely a technological means to reach a political end, an instrument for politics, but that it can be more than an instrument, that it *may have political value and interests itself*, and under certain conditions should be included in the political community. Here the claim is that AI politics should not only be politics by humans *for* non-humans (and humans) but also potentially politics *by* non-humans – with the "for whom" being an open question and potentially also including technological non-humans.

In philosophy of technology, this kind of question is usually formulated as a *moral* question: can machines have moral status? During the past two decades, there has been a lively debate on this topic in the ethics of AI and robotics community (e.g., Bostrom and Yudkowsky 2014; Coeckelbergh 2014; Danaher 2020; Darling 2016; Floridi and Sanders 2004; Gunkel 2018; Umbrello and Sorgner 2019). But what about the *political* status of such entities? What about their political rights, their freedom, their citizenship, justice with regard for how we relate to them, and so on?

Here are a number of interesting routes to explore some claims and arguments in this direction. A first way is to learn from the debate on the moral status of machines. Some of the discussion about political status will likely mirror that debate. For example, those who are unwilling to grant moral status to AI on the basis of a lack of properties such as consciousness or capacity for suffering will likely use the same argument for denying political status to AI. Others may argue that such intrinsic properties are not important for political status, and that, rather, the relational or communal dimension counts: if we relate to AI in social and communal ways, should that not be enough for giving some political status to these entities? For example, Gunkel (2018) and I (Coeckelbergh 2014) have questioned ascribing moral status on the basis of intrinsic properties and have suggested that where to draw the line is a political question of (re)negotiation and linked to a human history of exclusion and power, which should make us cautious regarding ascribing moral status to other entities now. The same could be said, *a fortiori*, for political status. Is it time to renegotiate the exclusion of machines from politics? A distinction that is also relevant to political status is that between moral agency and moral patiency: moral agency is about what AI should (not) do towards others, whereas moral patiency is about what could be done to AI. A similar distinction could be made between the political agency of AI and the political patiency of AI. For example, one could ask if AI has the properties required for political judgment and participation (agency), or what is *due to* AI, politically, under certain conditions (patiency).

An interesting connection between this discussion about moral status and political (and legal) philosophy can be made by focusing on the concept of rights. Gunkel's *Robot Rights* (2018), which discusses the moral and legal standing of robots in order to examine their social situation, is an excellent starting point for this exercise. As well as offering a helpful classification on different positions on robot rights, Gunkel goes beyond anthropocentrism by pointing out that rights do not necessarily mean *human* rights, and that we mistakenly believe that we know what we are talking about when we use the word "rights." There are different types of rights, such as privileges, claims, powers, and immunities. While most people will reject giving robots or AI *human* rights, one could use this analysis and try to argue for a particular type of right for machines that is less than, or different from, human rights, and consider their *political* significance. The recognition that rights need not be human rights or human-level rights opens up some space to do this. However, such a project would not only be rejected by those who *a priori* oppose the very idea of robot rights; it might also face relational objections. In line with critical posthumanism and postmodernism, it could be argued (Coeckelbergh 2014; Gunkel 2018) that this kind of reasoning itself constitutes a form of totalizing philosophy, which puts moral and political philosophy on a kind of platform from which entities are categorized and given rights – moral and political. Note also that drawing on Roman law in order to give robots a political status comparable to slaves, or more generally modeling a political rights framework on Roman legal categories of rights and citizenship, would be equally, if not more, problematic – also from a Marxian, postcolonial, and identity politics point of view (see chapter 3).

Another route is to take the arguments concerning the political status of animals and the environment and try to apply them to AI, for instance those that link political status to cooperation or intrinsic value (see the first section of this chapter). If consciousness or sentience is seen as an intrinsic property that warrants moral or political status in the case of animals, then if an artificially intelligent entity were to display the same property, we would have to give it the same status. If AI, like some animals, were to count as having interests or as acting as a cooperating partner in a cooperative scheme, then, according to, for instance, the arguments by Donaldson and Kymlicka (2011), it could be considered for political status, even if it is not conscious or sentient (but note that there are considerable debates about what counts as sentience). And if certain non-human entities such as rivers or rocks can be granted political status on the basis of their intrinsic value, without having to be conscious or sentient, then could some kinds of AI or "ecologies" of AI receive a similar status, especially if they were perceived as sacred or especially valuable by a particular community? Moreover, given the possibilities of synthetic biology and bioengineering, the boundary between living and non-living entities is becoming increasingly blurred. The labs of the scientists produce hybrids: between organism and artificial entity. In the future, we may have more "synthetic organisms" and "living machines" (Deplazes and Huppenbauer 2009). For example, bioengineers try to produce programmable cells. The cells seem alive, and at the same time they are machines since they are designed. If and to the extent that AI moves in the direction of "life" (e.g., becomes a "living machine"), then if life itself is seen as a sufficient condition for political status (e.g., political patiency), it would fulfill at least to some extent the same conditions for political status as (other) living beings. And how important is the category "life" anyway? If species and particular natural environments are valuable in themselves and if that affords political rights, as is argued by some environmentalists, then should "artificial species" and "artificial environments" (Owe, Baum, and Coeckelbergh forthcoming) also be protected, politically, if they fulfill similar functions and are perceived as intrinsically valuable? Posthumanists may also welcome all kinds of hybrids into the political community. For them, living machines and artificial life are not a problem; instead, holding on to the old life/non-life dualism is problematic, and destabilizing such dualisms and borders is part of their philosophical and indeed *political* project.

Like some arguments about the moral status of machines, some arguments about political status may be encouraged by recent successes in AI where it outperformed humans (e.g., in chess and in Go) and may assume that in the future humans may develop artificial general intelligence (AGI) or superintelligence (ASI). Transhumanists such as Bostrom (2014), Kurzweil (2005), and Moravec (1988) seriously consider this possibility and discuss scenarios in which greater-than-human intelligences emerge, colonize the earth, and then spread out into the universe. With regard to such scenarios, the political question does not only concern the political status of these superintelligent entities (as political agents or patients), but also the political status of humans: will superintelligent AI take over political power from humans, and what does that mean for the political status of humans? Will humans be the slaves of their artificial masters, as some animals are now the slaves of humans? Will humans be used as biological material or sources of energy (as we now do with some plants or animals – see also the film *The Matrix*) or be uploaded into the digital domain? Will they even still exist? What are the existential risks for humanity (Bostrom 2014), with "existential" used here in the sense that humanity might be destroyed? Can we give AI goals that are compatible with human goals, or will it change these goals and pursue its own, rather than humanity's, interests? The first option is favored by transhumanists such as Hughes (2004), who (in contrast to posthumanists) aim to continue and radicalize not only the Enlightenment but also humanism and democracy, even if the human is to be radically altered (Ferrando 2019, 33). Others believe that the human must be completely overcome and that we better make space for more intelligent beings than us. In any case, transhumanists agree that technologies such as AI, rather than education and human culture, will and should create better humans and more-than-humans, and that this will have political consequences for humanity as a whole in the sense that it will likely shift the power balance between humans (if any left) and their enhanced or superintelligent masters. Democracy and other old institutions may no longer be needed then, as Harari (2015) has suggested. While most transhumanists spend less time thinking about the more immediate political consequences for concrete humans and human societies, there are also branches of transhumanism that are explicitly political and concerned with the present, ranging from libertarian (Zoltan Istvan, who ran for US president in the 2016 elections) to democratic and leftist, calling attention to social issues (James Hughes).

Less futuristic and already relevant today is the role of AI in politics and governance as a political agent. Consider again the issue of political expertise and leadership: what kind of judgment and capacities are needed for politics, and how can we balance technocracy and democracy? If humans bring their judgment to bear upon challenging political issues, and if this capacity is related to their autonomy and normative status, could AI develop such a capacity for judgment, and hence acquire political agency? *Could* AI take over politics from humans? Would it have the kind of knowledge, expertise, and skills required for political leadership? And would such a role for AI in politics be compatible with democracy? Some of these questions have already been discussed in chapter 4, but now our concern is no longer merely with the instrumental role of AI with regard to knowledge, technocracy, and democracy, but rather with whether and how it can acquire its own political agency.

In order to answer this question, one could loop back to the discussion about the moral status and in particular the moral agency of non-humans (e.g., Floridi and Sanders again), but one could also elaborate on this discussion by once more considering posthumanist thinking about non-humans (Latour) or, like in chapter 4, by referring to political theory about leadership and citizenship, about whether rational capacities are needed, what the role of emotions is, what political expertise is, and so on. Consider, for example, Arendt's warning that common sense, thinking, and judgment are necessary in politics; following my suggestions in chapters 2 and 4, one could raise doubts about whether AI could acquire these capacities.

In addition to the "could" question there is, of course, also the "should" question. Few authors are openly enthusiastic about the possibility of AI technocracy. Even within the transhumanist literature, technocracy is sometimes rejected. Most prominently, Hughes has argued in *Citizen Cyborg* (2004) that technology should be under our democratic control. As well as reason, science and technology, we need democracy. More than this, Hughes urges, technological mastery over nature "requires radical democratization" (3). He calls for a democratic form of transhumanism and superintelligence: we will give birth to other forms of intelligence, but we should now "end war, inequality, poverty, disease, and unnecessary death" because this will determine the shape of that transhumanist future (xx). Furthermore, the idea that current humans will design what human beings will be in the future raises issues concerning transgenerational justice which are relevant to the here and now: do we want such a responsibility? Nevertheless, many transhumanists prefer to focus on the distant future, one that does not necessarily take place on this earth and with humanity as we know it. Today, tech billionaires such as Elon Musk and Jeff Bezos seem to support such visions and make plans to colonize space.

Some posthumanist theory touches upon the idea of the political status of machines and enlarging the political community to machines. In the previous section, I already noted how Haraway argues for a politics that crosses the organism/machine boundary and the biological species/technology boundary, against hegemonic orders and binaries. This is relevant not only for the political status of animals but also for the political status of machines. The cyborg metaphor is meant to deconstruct the human/machine dualism. Haraway expresses a posthumanist and "a feminist politics that embraces its entanglement with new technologies" (Atanasoski and Vora 2019, 81). However, here too, the point is not just that we need to think differently about technologies; we also need to rethink humans and politics. Gray (2000) takes up Haraway's cyborg imaginary in *Cyborg Citizen* (2000). The term refers to the observation that humans as a species continue to technologically transform themselves; in this sense, we are cyborgs. The question is then: what would a "cyborg society" (2) mean? What could citizenship mean in "the age of electronic reproduction" (21)? The author claims that technologies are political and that the technological order must be made more democratic (198). Since knowledge is power, cyborg citizens need to have information to govern. We also need new political institutions when new technologies are being developed.

Like Haraway, Barad (2015) has an interest in new political imaginaries. Drawing on Shelley's *Frankenstein* and queer and trans theories, she argues that monsters can invite us to explore new forms of becoming and kinship (410) and imagines a fusion with the non-human and posthuman other. In *Meeting the Universe Halfway* (2007), she questions dividing the world into categories such as the social and the natural. Using quantum mechanics as a source for her metaphors, she argues that instead we should "theorize the social and the natural together" (24–5). She tries to do this with her version of realism, agential realism, which also responds to a performative understanding of discursive practices (see again Butler). According to Barad, there are human and non-human forms of agency. She connects this with a notion of power inspired by Foucault and Butler, but (inspired by Fernandes) she also talks about relations of production, which are reconfigured by machinic agency. Machines and humans emerge through "specific entanglements of agencies" (239). They constitute one another. Elsewhere, Barad (2003) criticizes representationalism and links it with political individualism. Her alternative is the notion of posthumanist performativity, which calls into question categories such as human/non-human (808) or social/material, and understands power not only as social but also as working in materializations (810). Both human and non-human bodies "come to matter" through performativity and "agential intra-actions" (823–4).

Based on such approaches, many of the phenomena discussed in the previous chapters can be reframed as involving not only humans but also non-humans. The production of bias, inequality, and totalitarian forms of control and surveillance can be theorized as relying not only on humans but also on non-humans, including technologies and institutions. For example, influenced by Deleuze and Guattari, Haggerty and Ericson (2000) have argued that instead of using the metaphor of the panopticon to describe contemporary surveillance, we should use the term "surveillant assemblage" since it involves both humans and non-humans.

Another, somewhat posthumanist and certainly deconstructivist approach to human/non-human dualism with regard to AI is to say that questioning the human/AI distinction is not about questioning two terms that are fixed; in the process, the two also change. When we discuss what we mean by AI, we are not only discussing a technology but we are also using and discussing a metaphor: using the term "artificial intelligence" relies on a comparison with human intelligence. Now metaphors tend to change the two terms they connect. Inspired by Ricoeur's view on metaphor and in particular his term "predicative assimilation," which posits that metaphor generates "new bonds of resemblance that did not exist prior to the metaphoric union" (Ricoeur 1978, 148), Rhee (2018, 10–11) has identified a "metaphoric collapse" between humans and machines with regard to AI: anthropomorphization of AI creates a human that did not exist prior to humanization. In other words, AI makes us think differently not only about machines but about humans too. This also has political implications. Following Rhee, we can say that deciding how to shape the relation between humans and AI is an act of power. The creation and use of the term "AI" are themselves political acts in this sense. Metaphors also promote specific beliefs. For example, Broussard (2019) has argued that the term "machine learning" suggests that computers have agency and are sentient because they learn. Such a "linguistic confusion" (89) can also be seen as a (performative) exercise of power.

Sometimes posthumanism makes an explicit connection to political theory. Zolkos (2018) sees a posthuman turn in political theory which entails a non-anthropocentric theorizing of politics. This means, among other things, that biological organisms and machines are considered in terms of their political agency. For example, Lazzarato (2014) brings together the symbolic (signs) and the technological (machines). Machines are social actors, and mega-machines (a term borrowed from philosopher of technology Lewis Mumford) are assemblages that include humans, non-human animals, and inanimate objects. Lazzarato argues that in late capitalism, humans are subjected to the workings of mega-machines. Politics, then, not only is a matter of humans but additionally happens inside the (mega-) machine, where humans but also machines, objects, and signs are agents, and through which subjectivity is produced. As they "suggest, enable, solicit, prompt, encourage, and prohibit certain actions, thoughts, and affects" (30), machines establish power relations – the kind of power relations Foucault theorized. In particular, Lazzarato sees machinic *enslavement*: "the mode in which science, economics, communications networks, and the welfare state function" (31). He criticizes neoliberalism and sees the possibility of radical political change in interruptive events.

But can transhumanism and even posthumanism sufficiently support such a change and take up a critical role? From a critical theory point of view, one could look at this entire discussion about the moral and political status of AI as science-fiction narratives and performances that risk supporting the use and development of AI for generating profit for the few by means of capitalist exploitation. In the previous chapter, on power, I gave the example of the humanoid robot Sophia: its performances and narratives appeal to the idea of political status (citizenship), but – so a critical theorist could argue – this is really about making profit and accumulating capital. We should absolutely discuss the impact of AI on human beings and perhaps also non-humans. But to talk about the political status of AI (as agents or patients) may distract from forms of capitalist exploitation that are bad for people and the (rest of the) planet.

Finally, as posthumanists, environmentalists, and feminists remind us, talk about the future of "humanity" and our relation to "nature," or even about non-human, machine "others" (as in the work of some posthumanists), may well distract us from politics at the level of the domestic and personal sphere: the "small" politics that is linked with "big" politics. What we do with AI and with one another in everyday life is also political (and, as the discussions on equality and power in the previous chapters show, how we define that "we" is political). The politics of AI reaches deep down into what you and I do with technology at home, in the workplace, with friends, and so on, which in turn shapes that politics. Perhaps this is the real power of AI: by what we do on our smartphones and our other screens in everyday life(worlds), we actually give power to AI and those who use it for capital accumulation, support specific hegemonic societal structures, reinforce binaries, and deny pluralities. In this sense, too, "data is the new oil": neither data nor oil would be so important if we didn't use it, if we were not addicted to it. Again, AI and the politics of AI are about people: people who have an interest in keeping us addicted. At the same time, this also opens up possibilities for resistance and change.

7

Conclusion: Political Technologies

What I have done in this book and what we can conclude

In response to normative issues raised by AI and related technologies, this book has argued that when it comes to using resources from practical philosophy, it is helpful to use not only ethics but also political philosophy. In each chapter, I have made suggestions for how to create bridges between AI and political philosophy by focusing on specific political principles and problems and relating them to AI. It has become clear that the issues we currently care about in political and societal discussions, such as freedom, racism, justice, power, and (threats to) democracy, take on a new urgency and meaning in the light of technological developments such as AI and robotics, and that political philosophy can help to conceptualize and discuss these issues and meanings. The book shows how theory about freedom, justice, equality, democracy, power, and non-anthropocentric politics can be productively used for thinking about AI.

More precisely, I have undertaken a twofold exercise. On the one hand, I have shown how concepts and theory from political philosophy and social theory can help us to frame, understand, and approach the normative-political challenges raised by AI. This has led to a sketch of *a political philosophy of AI*, which is *one* kind of conceptual toolbox that can help us to think about the politics of AI. It is not meant to be exclusive; I welcome efforts from other directions, and some of the literature cited does not come from political philosophy, strictly speaking. Moreover, the book is meant as an introduction, leaving plenty of room for further work on each of these topics. Nevertheless, it *offers some substantial building blocks for an evaluative, normative framework for thinking about the political aspects of AI*, which may be useful for those who are interested in the normative aspects of AI in research, higher education, business, and policy. I hope its conceptual tools and discourse not only are academically interesting but may also guide actual efforts to deal with the challenges raised by what turns out to be artificial intelligence *and* artificial *power*: AI is both technological and *political*.

On the other hand, alongside this practical use, this exercise in *applied political philosophy* of AI also has philosophical significance that goes beyond application: it turned out that conceptualizing the politics of AI and robotics is not a matter of simply applying existing notions from political philosophy and social theory, but *invites us to question the very concepts and values themselves* (freedom, equality, justice, democracy, power, human-centered politics) and to revisit interesting questions about the nature and future of politics. For example, what is and should be the role of expertise, rationality, and emotions in politics? And what does a post-anthropocentric politics mean, once we question the central and hegemonic position of humans? The book shows that discussions about AI invite us, in a sense "force" us, to revisit political-philosophical concepts and discussions, and in the end also challenge us to question the human and humanism – or at least some problematic versions of these concepts.

In the light of this experience that thinking about technology tickles and sometimes destabilizes our thinking about politics, I suggest that political philosophy in the 21st century can no longer be done, and should no longer be done, without responding to the question concerning technology. We have to *zusammendenken* ("think together") politics and technology: thinking about the one cannot be done without thinking about the other. More dialogue between these fields of thinking is urgently needed and, perhaps ultimately, there should be a merging of the two.

And it is high time we did this. Like all philosophy, according to Hegel, who said in 1820 in his *Outlines of the Philosophy of Right* that philosophy is "its own time apprehended in thoughts" (Hegel 2008, 15), political philosophy should respond to and reflect its time, and perhaps cannot do anything else than respond to and reflect its time, cannot really transcend its time. To paraphrase the Latin maxim cited by Hegel: here is where we have to jump; it's time for a *salto mortale*. And our time is not only a time of societal, environmental, and existential-psychological unrest and transformation; it is also a time in which new *technologies* such as AI are closely entangled with these changes and developments. It is the time of AI. Thinking about the future of politics, then, needs to crucially be connected to thinking about technologies and their relation to politics. In this case: AI is here, AI is (of) our time, and hence *AI is where we have to jump and think.* Based on political philosophy and related relevant theory (e.g., social theory about power, posthumanist theory), this book has provided some guidance for this jumping and thinking.

However, this is just the beginning, a first step or prolegomenon, if you wish: a critical introduction to a larger project concerning politics and AI, and more generally politics and technology. Let me end this book by offering a sense of the work that lies ahead.

What needs to be done next: The question regarding political technologies

As an introduction and as a philosophy book, the focus of this volume has been on asking the questions rather than providing answers. It has offered suggestions for how political philosophy can help, which have grown into a toolbox and a framework, a structure that assists to discuss the politics of AI. However, more work is required. More precisely, there are at least two kinds of next steps needed.

First, more research and thinking are needed to further develop the framework. It is like a scaffold: it is supportive but temporary, and what is needed now is further construction. As the literature on the politics of AI is rapidly growing, I have no doubt that more building will be done on issues such as bias in AI, the power of big tech, AI and democracy, and so on. But in the light of the project of this book, which concerns assisting the birth of a *political philosophy* of AI, I hope especially that (1) more *philosophers* will write about the politics of AI (currently it is often done by people from other disciplines and there is a lot of non-academic writing that does little more than scratch the surface) and that (2) more work will be done using *political philosophy* and social theory, whose resources are currently heavily under-used in normative thinking about AI and in philosophy of technology, perhaps because they are less familiar or less popular than ethics. As Langdon Winner, a prominent philosopher of technology, already argued in the 1980s: technology is political. He warned that instead of bringing about more democratization and social equality, new technologies may well lead to more power for those who already have a great deal of it (Winner 1986, 107). As my book shows, by using the resources of political philosophy, we can further develop the idea that technology is political and critically discuss the impact of technologies such as AI.

Second, if politics is to be defined as something that is by definition of public concern and in which we should all participate, thinking about the politics of AI should also take place outside academia and should be done by all kinds of stakeholders and in all kinds of contexts. The politics of AI is not something that we should only think about and write about in books; it is something that we should also *do*. If we reject the Platonic idea that only philosophers and experts should rule, then finding out what the good society is in the light of AI is something that we should find out together: the politics of AI should be publicly discussed and participatory, and this should be done in an inclusive way. But this does not exclude a role for philosophy and philosophers: concepts and theories from political philosophy as offered in this book may help to raise the quality of such public discussions. For example, today it is often said that AI threatens democracy, but it is unclear why and what is meant by democracy. As I showed in chapter 4, political philosophy, with assistance from philosophy of technology and media, can help to clarify this. Moreover, given some of the dangers indicated in this book (e.g., biases and forms of discrimination in society; echo chambers and filter bubbles via social media; the danger of totalitarian use of AI), we face the challenge of *how* to tackle these challenges and how to improve the discussion. What procedures, infrastructures, and forms of knowledge do we need for a democratic and inclusive discussion about AI and other technologies? And, indeed, what *technologies* do we (not) need and how do we best (not) use them? What kind of social media do we need, and what should be the role and place of AI, if any? Thinking about how to do the politics of AI in a democratic and inclusive way leads us back to one of the basic questions we should ask about democracy and politics itself: *how* to do it. And if the question concerning politics and the question concerning technology are indeed that connected, then this question can also be formulated as: what *political technologies* do we need and want?

Finally, to the extent that this book has used, and responded to, standard anglophone political philosophy, the presented framework has also partly borrowed its biases, cultural-political orientations, and limitations. For example, many discussions I encountered during my journey through the English-speaking political-philosophical landscape simply take for granted the political context and culture of the US, thereby ignoring other approaches and contexts in other parts of the world and – arguably worse – ignoring *how their philosophical views, arguments, and assumptions are shaped by their own political-cultural context.* Furthermore, most modern political philosophy is focused on the context of the nation state and fails to address challenges that arise in a global context. When it comes to the further development of both academic and non-academic thinking about AI and politics, it will be vital to address those issues and navigate the challenges raised by the politics of AI in ways that take into account the *global* context in which these issues arise and create sufficient sensitivity to the *cultural differences* with regard to the way different people and cultures think about technology, about politics, and indeed about humans. First, given that AI does not stop at the border and has an impact that goes beyond nation states, and given that there are many different AI actors in the world (not only the US but also Europe, China, etc.), it is important to think about the politics of AI in a global context and perhaps develop a global politics of AI. Such a project raises its own challenges. For example, various inter-governmental and non-governmental organizations are already developing policies for dealing with AI. But is this *inter*national work – between nations – sufficient or do we need (more) *supra*national forms of governance? Do we need new political institutions, new political technologies to govern AI at a global level? *What global political technologies do we need?* Second, it must be borne in mind that the literatures offered in this book reflect specific political contexts. For example, when Eubanks (2018) criticizes a specific moralistic way of dealing with poverty, this criticism is situated within a US political culture, which is not necessarily shared by other countries, and which has its own challenges related to *that* political culture. Thinking about the politics of AI will need to become more sensitive to this dimension of cultural difference, especially if it seeks to become more relational, more imaginative, more responsible, and more practically relevant in both local and global contexts.

To conclude, this book embodies not only a recommendation to use political philosophy for thinking about AI; more generally and more ambitiously, it is also an invitation to risk this *salto mortale* of thinking together politics and technology, and to do this in a way that responds to what is happening in our societies and in the world. It is time to do so, and it is much needed. If we do not take this route, we will not achieve sufficient critical and reflective distance from what technologies such as AI are already doing to us and to politics, and we will be the helpless victims of artificial intelligence and artificial power. That is, we will be the helpless victims of ourselves and our society: of the very human – all too human – technologies, metaphors, dualisms, and power structures that we allow to rule us. This evokes the dystopian narratives and, unfortunately, real-world examples that came up time and again over the course of this book: stories and cases that displayed how key political principles and values have come under threat. We can and should do better. Thinking about political technologies, which connects thinking about technology to questioning the fundamental principles and structures of our societies and the global political order, can help us to create and live better, more positive stories – not about a distant future but in the here and now. Stories about AI, about us, and about other beings and things that matter.

References

Aavitsland, V. L. (2019). "The Failure of Judgment: Disgust in Arendt's Theory of Political Judgment." *Journal of Speculative Philosophy* 33(3), pp. 537–50.

Adorno, T. (1983). *Prisms*. Translated by S. Weber and S. Weber. Cambridge, MA: MIT Press.

Agamben, G. (1998). *Homo Sacer: Sovereign Power and Bare Life*. Translated by D. Heller-Roazen. Stanford: Stanford University Press.

AI Institute. (2019). "AI and Climate Change: How They're Connected, and What We Can Do about It." *Medium*, October 17. Available at: https://medium.com/@AINowInstitute/ai-and-climate-change-how-theyre-connected-and-what-we-can-do-about-it-6aa8d0f5b32c

Alaimo, S. (2016). *Exposed: Environmental Politics and Pleasures in Posthuman Times*. Minneapolis: University of Minnesota Press.

Albrechtslund, A. (2008). "Online Social Networking as Participatory Surveillance." *First Monday* 13(3). Available at: https://doi.org/10.5210/fm.v13i3.2142

Andrejevic, M. (2020). *Automated Media*. New York: Routledge.

Arendt, H. (1943). "We Refugees." *Menorah Journal* 31(1), pp. 69–77.

Arendt, H. (1958). *The Human Condition*. Chicago: University of Chicago Press.

Arendt, H. (1968). *Between Past and Future*. New York: Viking Press.

Arendt, H. (2006). *Eichmann in Jerusalem: A Report on the Banality of Evil*. New York: Penguin.

Arendt, H. (2017). *The Origins of Totalitarianism*. London: Penguin.

Asdal, K., Druglitrø, T., and Hinchliffe, S. (2017). "Introduction: The 'More-Than-Human' Condition." In K. Asdal, T. Druglitrø, T., and

S. Hinchliffe (eds.), *Humans, Animals, and Biopolitics*. Abingdon: Routledge, pp. 1–29.

Atanasoski, N., and Vora, K. (2019). *Surrogate Humanity: Race, Robots, and the Politics of Technological Futures*. Durham, NC: Duke University Press.

Austin, J. L. (1962). *How to Do Things with Words*. Cambridge, MA: Harvard University Press.

Azmanova, A. (2020). *Capitalism on Edge: How Fighting Precarity Can Achieve Radical Change without Crisis or Utopia*. New York: Columbia University Press.

Bakardjieva, M., and Gaden, G. (2011). "Web 2.0 Technologies of the Self." *Philosophy & Technology* 25, pp. 399–413.

Barad, K. (2003). "Posthumanist Performativity: Towards an Understanding of How Matter Comes to Matter." *Signs: Journal of Women in Culture and Society* 28(3), pp. 801–31.

Barad, K. (2007). *Meeting the Universe Halfway: Quantum Physics and the Entanglement of Matter and Meaning*. Durham, NC: Duke University Press.

Barad, K. (2015). "Transmaterialities: Trans*Matter/Realities and Queer Political Imaginings." *GLQ: A Journal of Lesbian and Gay Studies* 21(2–3), pp. 387–422.

Bartneck, C., Lütge, C., Wagner, A., and Welsh, S. (2021). *An Introduction to Ethics in Robotics and AI*. Cham: Springer.

Bartoletti, I. (2020). *An Artificial Revolution: On Power, Politics and AI*. London: The Indigo Press. BBC (2018). "Fitbit Data Used to Charge US Man with Murder." *BBC News*, October 4. Available at: https://www.bbc.com/news/technology-45745366.

Bell, D. A. (2016). *The China Model: Political Meritocracy and the Limits of Democracy*. Princeton: Princeton University Press.

Benjamin, R. (2019a). *Race After Technology*. Cambridge: Polity.

Benjamin, R. (2019b). *Captivating Technology: Race, Carceral Technoscience, and Liberatory Imagination in Everyday Life*. Durham, NC: Duke University Press.

Berardi, F. (2017). *Futurability: The Age of Impotence and the Horizon of Possibility*. London: Verso.

Berlin, I. (1997). "Two Concepts of Liberty." In: I. Berlin, *The Proper Study of Mankind*. London: Chatto & Windus, pp. 191–242.

Berman, J. (2011). "Futurist Ray Kurzweil Says He Can Bring His Dead Father Back to Life Through a Computer Avatar." *ABC News*, August 10. Available at: https://abcnews.go.com/Technology/futurist-ray-kurzweil-bring-dead-father-back-life/story?id=14267712

Bernal, N. (2020). "They Claim Uber's Algorithm Fired Them. Now They're Taking It to Court." *Wired*, November 2. Available at: https://www.wired.co.uk/article/uber-fired-algorithm

Bietti, E. (2020). "Consent as a Free Pass: Platform Power and the Limits of Information Turn." *Pace Law Review* 40(1), pp. 310–98.

Binns, R. (2018). "Fairness in Machine Learning: Lessons from Political Philosophy." Proceedings of the 1st Conference on Fairness, Accountability and Transparency. *Proceedings of Machine Learning Research* 81, pp. 149–59. Available at: http://proceedings.mlr.press/v81/binns18a.html

Birhane, A. (2020). "Algorithmic Colonization of Africa." *SCRIPTed: A Journal of Law, Technology, & Society* 17(2). Available at: https://script-ed.org/article/algorithmic-colonization-of-africa/

Bloom, P. (2019). *Monitored: Business and Surveillance in a Time of Big Data.* London: Pluto Press.

Boddington, P. (2017). *Towards a Code of Ethics of Artificial Intelligence.* Cham: Springer.

Bostrom, N. (2014). *Superintelligence: Paths, Dangers, Strategies.* Oxford: Oxford University Press.

Bostrom, N., and Yudkowsky, E. (2014). "The Ethics of Artificial Intelligence." In: K. Frankish and W. Ramsey (eds.), *Cambridge Handbook of Artificial Intelligence.* New York: Cambridge University Press, pp. 316–34.

Bourdieu, P. (1990). *The Logic of Practice.* Translated by R. Nice. Stanford: Stanford University Press.

Bozdag, E. (2013). "Bias in Algorithmic Filtering and Personalization." *Ethics and Information Technology* 15(3), pp. 209–27.

Bradley, A. (2011). *Originary Technicity: The Theory of Technology from Marx to Derrida.* Basingstoke: Palgrave Macmillan.

Braidotti, R. (2016). "Posthuman Critical Theory." In: D. Banerji and M. Paranjape (eds.), *Critical Posthumanism and Planetary Futures.* New Delhi: Springer, pp. 13–32.

Braidotti, R. (2017). "Posthuman Critical Theory." *Journal of Posthuman Studies* 1(1), pp. 9–25.

Braidotti, R. (2020). "'We' Are in This Together, but We Are Not One and the Same." *Journal of Bioethical Inquiry* 17(4), pp. 465–9.

Broussard, M. (2019). *Artificial Unintelligence: How Computers Misunderstand the World.* Cambridge, MA: MIT Press.

Bryson, J. J. (2010). "Robots Should Be Slaves." In: Y. Wilks (ed.), *Close Engagements with Artificial Companions.* Amsterdam: John Benjamins Publishing, pp. 63–74.

Butler, J. (1988). "Performative Acts and Gender Constitution: An Essay in Phenomenology and Feminist Theory." *Theatre Journal* 40(4), pp. 519–31.

Butler, J. (1989). "Foucault and the Paradox of Bodily Inscriptions." *Journal of Philosophy* 86(11), pp. 601–7.

Butler, J. (1993). *Bodies That Matter: On the Discursive Limits of "Sex."* London: Routledge.

Butler, J. (1997). *Excitable Speech: A Politics of the Performative*. New York: Routledge.

Butler, J. (1999). *Gender Trouble: Feminism and the Subversion of Identity*. New York: Routledge.

Butler, J. (2004). *Precarious life: The Powers of Mourning and Violence*. London: Verso.

Caliskan, A., Bryson, J. J., and Narayanan, A. (2017). "Semantics Derived Automatically from Language Corpora Contain Human-Like Biases." *Science* 356(6334), pp. 183–6.

Callicott, J. B. (1989). *In Defense of the Land Ethic: Essays in Environmental Philosophy*. Albany: State University of New York Press.

Canavan, G. (2015). "Capital as Artificial Intelligence." *Journal of American Studies* 49(4), pp. 685–709.

Castells, M. (2001). *The Internet Galaxy: Reflections on the Internet, Business, and Society*. Oxford: Oxford University Press.

Celermajer, D., Schlosberg, D., Rickards, L., Stewart-Harawira, M., Thaler, M., Tschakert, P., Verlie, B., and Winter, C. (2021). "Multispecies Justice: Theories, Challenges, and a Research Agenda for Environmental Politics." *Environmental Politics* 30(1–2), pp. 119–40.

Cheney-Lippold, J. (2017). *We Are Data: Algorithms and the Making of Our Digital Selves*. New York: New York University Press.

Chou, M., Moffitt, B., and Bryant, O. (2020). *Political Meritocracy and Populism: Cure or Curse?*. New York: Routledge.

Christiano, T. (ed.) (2003). *Philosophy and Democracy: An Anthology*. Oxford: Oxford University Press.

Christiano, T., and Bajaj, S. (2021). "Democracy." *Stanford Encyclopedia of Philosophy*. Available at: https://plato.stanford.edu/entries/democracy/

Christman, J. (2004). "Relational Autonomy, Liberal Individualism, and the Social Constitution of Selves." *Philosophical Studies* 117(1–2), pp. 143–64.

Coeckelbergh, M. (2009a). "The Public Thing: On the Idea of a Politics of Artefacts." *Techné* 13(3), pp. 175–81.

Coeckelbergh, M. (2009b). "Distributive Justice and Cooperation in a World of Humans and Non-Humans: A Contractarian Argument for Drawing Non-Humans into the Sphere of Justice." *Res Publica* 15(1), pp. 67–84.

Coeckelbergh, M. (2012). *Growing Moral Relations: Critique of Moral Status Ascription*. Basingstoke and New York: Palgrave Macmillan.

Coeckelbergh, M. (2013). *Human Being @ Risk*. Dordrecht: Springer.

Coeckelbergh, M. (2014). "The Moral Standing of Machines: Towards a Relational and Non-Cartesian Moral Hermeneutics." *Philosophy & Technology* 27(1), pp. 61–77.

Coeckelbergh, M. (2015a). "The Tragedy of the Master: Automation, Vulnerability, and Distance." *Ethics and Information Technology* 17(3), pp. 219–29.

Coeckelbergh, M. (2015b). *Environmental Skill*. Abingdon Routledge.

Coeckelbergh, M. (2017). "Beyond 'Nature'. Towards More Engaged and Care-Full Ways of Relating to the Environment." In: H. Kopnina and E. Shoreman-Ouimet (eds.), *Routledge Handbook of Environmental Anthropology*. Abingdon: Routledge, pp. 105–16.

Coeckelbergh, M. (2019a). *Introduction to Philosophy of Technology*. New York: Oxford University Press.

Coeckelbergh, M. (2019b). *Moved by Machines: Performance Metaphors and Philosophy of Technology*. New York: Routledge.

Coeckelbergh, M. (2019c). "Technoperformances: Using Metaphors from the Performance Arts for a Postphenomenology and Posthermeneutics of Technology Use." *AI & Society* 35(3), pp. 557–68.

Coeckelbergh, M. (2020). *AI Ethics*. Cambridge, MA: MIT Press.

Coeckelbergh, M. (2021). "How to Use Virtue Ethics for Thinking about the Moral Standing of Social Robots: A Relational Interpretation in Terms of Practices, Habits, and Performance." *International Journal of Social Robotics* 13(1), pp. 31–40.

Confavreux, J., and Rancière, J. (2020). "The Crisis of Democracy." *Verso*, February 24. Available at: https://www.versobooks.com/blogs/4576-jacques-ranciere-the-crisis-of-democracy

Cook, G., Lee, J., Tsai, T., Kong, A., Deans, J., Johnson, B., and Jardin, E. (2017). *Clicking Clean: Who Is Winning the Race to Build a Green Internet?* Washington: Greenpeace.

Cotter, K., and Reisdorf, B. C. (2020). "Algorithmic Knowledge Gaps: A New Dimension of (Digital) Inequality." *International Journal of Communication* 14, pp. 745–65.

Couldry, N., Livingstone, S., and Markham, T. (2007). *Media Consumption and Public Engagement: Beyond the Presumption of Attention*. New York: Palgrave Macmillan.

Couldry, N., and Mejias, U. A. (2019). *The Costs of Connection: How Data Is Colonizing Human Life and Appropriating It for Capitalism*. Stanford: Stanford University Press.

Crary, J. (2014). *24/7: Late Capitalism and the Ends of Sleep*. London: Verso.

Crawford, K. (2021). *Atlas of AI: Power, Politics, and the Planetary Costs of Artificial Intelligence*. New Haven: Yale University Press.

Crawford, K., and Calo, R. (2016). "There Is a Blind Spot in AI Research." *Nature* 538, pp. 311–13.

Criado Perez, C. (2019). *Invisible Women: Data Bias in a World Designed for Men*. New York: Abrams Press.

Crutzen, P. (2006). "The 'Anthropocene.'" In: E. Ehlers and T. Krafft (eds.), *Earth System Science in the Anthropocene*. Berlin: Springer, pp. 13–18.

Cudworth, E., and Hobden, S. (2018). *The Emancipatory Project of Posthumanism*. London: Routledge.

Curry, P. (2011). *Ecological Ethics. An Introduction*. Second edition. Cambridge: Polity.

Dahl, R.A. (2006). *A Preface to Democratic Theory*. Chicago: University of Chicago Press.

Damnjanović, I. (2015). "Polity without Politics? Artificial Intelligence versus Democracy: Lessons from Neal Asher's Polity Universe." *Bulletin of Science, Technology & Society* 35(3–4), pp. 76–83.

Danaher, J. (2020). "Welcoming Robots into the Moral Circle: A Defence of Ethical Behaviorism." *Science and Engineering Ethics* 26(4), pp. 2023–49.

Darling, K. (2016). "Extending Legal Protection to Social Robots: The Effects of Anthropomorphism, Empathy, and Violent Behavior towards Robotic Objects." In: R. Calo, A. M. Froomkin, and I. Kerr (eds.), *Robot Law*. Cheltenham: Edward Elgar Publishing, pp. 213–32.

Dauvergne, P. (2020). "The Globalization of Artificial Intelligence: Consequences for the Politics of Environmentalism." *Globalizations* 18(2), pp. 285–99.

Dean, J. (2009). *Democracy and Other Neoliberal Fantasies: Communicative Capitalism and Left Politics*. Durham, NC: Duke University Press.

Deleuze, G., and Guattari, F. (1987). *A Thousand Plateaus: Capitalism and Schizophrenia*. Translated by B. Massumi. Minneapolis: University of Minnesota Press.

Dent, N. (2005). *Rousseau*. London: Routledge.

Deplazes, A., and Huppenbauer, M. (2009). "Synthetic Organisms and Living Machines." *Systems and Synthetic Biology* 3(55). Available at: https://doi.org/10.1007/s11693-009-9029-4

Derrida, J. (1976). *Of Grammatology*. Translated by G. C. Spivak. Baltimore, MD: Johns Hopkins University Press.

Derrida, J. (1981). "Plato's Pharmacy." In J. Derrida, *Dissemination*. Translated by B. Johnson. Chicago: University of Chicago Press, pp. 63–171.

Detrow, S. (2018). "What Did Cambridge Analytica Do during the 2016 Election?" *NPR*, March 21. Available at: https://text.npr.org/595338116

Dewey, J. (2001). *Democracy and Education*. Hazleton, PA: Penn State Electronic Classics Series.

Diamond, L. (2019). "The Threat of Postmodern Totalitarianism." *Journal of Democracy* 30(1), pp. 20–4.

Dignum, V. (2019). *Responsible Artificial Intelligence*. Cham: Springer.

Dixon, S. (2007). *Digital Performance: A History of New Media in Theater, Dance, Performance Art, and Installation*. Cambridge, MA: MIT Press.

Djeffal, C. (2019). "AI, Democracy and the Law." In: A. Sudmann (ed.), *The Democratization of Artificial Intelligence: Net Politics in the Era of Learning Algorithms*. Bielefeld: Transcript, pp. 255–83.

Donaldson, S., and Kymlicka, W. (2011). *Zoopolis: A Political Theory of Animal Rights*. New York: Oxford University Press.

Downing, L. (2008). *The Cambridge Introduction to Michel Foucault*. New York: Cambridge University Press.

Dubber, M., Pasquale, F., and Das, S. (2020). *The Oxford Handbook of Ethics of AI*. Oxford: Oxford University Press.

Dworkin, R. (2011). *Justice for Hedgehogs*. Cambridge, MA: Belknap Press.

Dworkin, R. (2020). "Paternalism." *Stanford Encyclopedia of Philosophy*. Available at: https://plato.stanford.edu/entries/paternalism/

Dyer-Witheford, N. (1999). *Cyber-Marx: Cycles and Circuits of Struggle in High-Technology Capitalism*. Urbana: University of Illinois Press.

Dyer-Witheford, N. (2015). *Cyber-Proletariat Global Labour in the Digital Vortex*. London: Pluto Press.

Dyer-Witheford, N., Kjøsen, A. M., and Steinhoff, J. (2019). *Inhuman Power: Artificial Intelligence and the Future of Capitalism*. London: Pluto Press.

El-Bermawy, M. M. (2016). "Your Filter Bubble Is Destroying Democracy." *Wired*, November 18. Available at: https://www.wired.com/2016/11/filter-bubble-destroying-democracy/

Elkin-Koren, N. (2020). "Contesting Algorithms: Restoring the Public Interest in Content Filtering by Artificial Intelligence." *Big Data & Society* 7(2). Available at: https://doi.org/10.1177/2053951720932296

Eriksson, K. (2012). "Self-Service Society: Participative Politics and New Forms of Governance." *Public Administration* 90(3), pp. 685–98.

Eshun, K. (2003). "Further Considerations of Afrofuturism." *CR: The New Centennial Review* 3(2), pp. 287–302.

Estlund, D. (2008). *Democratic Authority: A Philosophical Framework*. Princeton: Princeton University Press.

Eubanks, V. (2018). *Automating Inequality: How High-Tech Tools Profile, Police, and Punish the Poor*. New York: St. Martin's Press.

Farkas, J. (2020). "A Case against the Post-Truth Era: Revisiting Mouffe's Critique of Consensus-Based Democracy." In: M. Zimdars and K. McLeod (eds.), *Fake News: Understanding Media and Misinformation in the Digital Age*. Cambridge, MA: MIT Press, pp. 45–54.

Farkas, J., and Schou, J. (2018). "Fake News as a Floating Signifier: Hegemony, Antagonism and the Politics of Falsehood." *Javnost – The Public* 25(3), pp. 298–314.

Farkas, J., and Schou, J. (2020). *Post-Truth, Fake News and Democracy: Mapping the Politics of Falsehood*. New York: Routledge.

Feenberg, A. (1991). *Critical Theory of Technology*. Oxford: Oxford University Press.

Feenberg, A. (1999). *Questioning Technology*. London: Routledge.

Ferrando, F. (2019). *Philosophical Posthumanism*. London: Bloomsbury Academic.

Floridi, L. (2013). *The Ethics of Information*. Oxford: Oxford University Press.

Floridi, L. (2014). *The Fourth Revolution*. Oxford: Oxford University Press.

Floridi, L. (2017). "Roman Law Offers a Better Guide to Robot Rights Than Sci-Fi." *Financial Times*, February 22. Available at: https://www.academia.edu/31710098/Roman_law_offers_a_better_guide_to_robot_rights_than_sci_fi

Floridi, L., and Sanders, J. W. (2004). "On the Morality of Artificial Agents." *Minds & Machines* 14(3), pp. 349–79.

Fogg, B. (2003). *Persuasive Technology: Using Computers to Change What We Think and Do*. San Francisco: Morgan Kaufmann.

Ford, M. (2015). *The Rise of the Robots: Technology and the Threat of a Jobless Future*. New York: Basic Books.

Foucault, M. (1977). *Discipline and Punish: The Birth of the Prison*. Translated by A. Sheridan. New York: Vintage Books.

Foucault, M. (1980). *Power/Knowledge: Selected Interviews and Other Writings 1972–1977*. Edited by C. Gordon, translated by C. Gordon, L. Marshall, J. Mepham, and K. Soper. New York: Pantheon Books.

Foucault, M. (1981). *History of Sexuality: Volume 1: An Introduction*. Translated by R. Hurley. London: Penguin.

Foucault, M. (1988). "Technologies of the Self". In: L. H. Martin, H. Gutman, and P. H. Hutton (eds.), *Technologies of the Self: A Seminar with Michel Foucault*. Amherst: University of Massachusetts Press, pp. 16–49.

Frankfurt, H. (2000). "Distinguished Lecture in Public Affairs: The Moral Irrelevance of Equality." *Public Affairs Quarterly* 14(2), pp. 87–103.

Frankfurt, H. (2015). *On Inequality*. Princeton: Princeton University Press.

Fuchs, C. (2014). *Social Media: A Critical Introduction*. London: Sage Publications.

Fuchs, C. (2020). *Communication and Capitalism: A Critical Theory*. London: University of Westminster Press.

Fuchs, C., Boersma, K., Albrechtslund, A., and Sandoval, M. (eds.) (2012). *Internet and Surveillance: The Challenges of Web 2.0 and Social Media*. London: Routledge.

Fukuyama, F. (2006). "Identity, Immigration, and Liberal Democracy." *Journal of Democracy* 17(2), pp. 5–20.

Fukuyama, F. (2018a). "Against Identity Politics: The New Tribalism and the Crisis of Democracy." *Foreign Affairs* 97(5), pp. 90–115.

Fukuyama, F. (2018b). *Identity: The Demand for Dignity and the Politics of Resentment*. New York: Farrar, Straus and Giroux.

Gabriels, K., and Coeckelbergh, M. (2019). "Technologies of the Self and the Other: How Self-Tracking Technologies Also Shape the Other." *Journal of Information, Communication and Ethics in Society* 17(2). Available at: https://doi.org/10.1108/JICES-12-2018-0094

Garner, R. (2003). "Animals, Politics, and Justice: Rawlsian Liberalism and the Plight of Non-Humans." *Environmental Politics* 12(2), pp. 3–22.

Garner, R. (2012). "Rawls, Animals and Justice: New Literature, Same Response." *Res Publica* 18(2), pp. 159–72.

Gellers, J. C. (2020). "Earth System Governance Law and the Legal Status of Non-Humans in the Anthropocene." *Earth System Governance* 7. Available at: https://doi.org/10.1016/j.esg.2020.100083

Giebler, H., and Merkel, W. (2016). "Freedom and Equality in Democracies: Is There a Trade-Off?" *International Political Science Review* 37(5), pp. 594–605.

Gilley, B. (2016). "Technocracy and Democracy as Spheres of Justice in Public Policy." *Policy Sciences* 50(1), pp. 9–22.

Gitelman, L., and Jackson, V. (2013). "Introduction." In L. Gitelman (ed.), *"Raw Data" Is an Oxymoron*. Cambridge, MA: MIT Press, pp. 1–14.

Goodin, R. E. (2003). *Reflective Democracy*. Oxford: Oxford University Press.

Gorwa, R., Binns, R., and Katzenbach, C. (2020). "Algorithmic Content Moderation: Technical and Political Challenges in the Automation of Platform Governance." *Big Data & Society* 7(1). Available at: https://doi.org/10.1177/2053951719897945.

Granka, L. A. (2010). "The Politics of Search: A Decade Retrospective." *The Information Society Journal* 26(5), pp. 364–74.

Gray, C. H. (2000). *Cyborg Citizen: Politics in the Posthuman Age*. London: Routledge.

Gunkel, D. (2014). "A Vindication of the Rights of Machines." *Philosophy & Technology* 27(1), pp. 113–32.

Gunkel, D. (2018). *Robot Rights*. Cambridge, MA: MIT Press.

Habermas, J. (1990). *Moral Consciousness and Communicative Action*. Translated by C. Lenhart and S. W. Nicholson. Cambridge, MA: MIT Press.

Hacker, P. (2018). "Teaching Fairness to Artificial Intelligence: Existing and Novel Strategies against Algorithmic Discrimination under EU Law." *Common Market Law Review* 55(4), pp. 1143–85.

Haggerty, K., and Ericson, R. (2000). "The Surveillant Assemblage." *British Journal of Sociology* 51(4), pp. 605–22.

Han, B.-C. (2015). *The Burnout Society*. Stanford: Stanford University Press.

Harari, Y. N. (2015). *Homo Deus: A Brief History of Tomorrow*. London: Harvill Secker.

Haraway, D. (2000). "A Cyborg Manifesto." In: D. Bell and B. M. Kennedy (eds.), *The Cybercultures Reader*. London: Routledge, pp. 291–324.

Haraway, D. (2003). *The Companion Species Manifesto: Dogs, People, and Significant Otherness*. Chicago: Prickly Paradigm Press.

Haraway, D. (2015). "Anthropocene, Capitalocene, Plantationocene, Chthulucene: Making Kin." *Environmental Humanities* 6, pp. 159–65.

Haraway, D. (2016). *Staying with the Trouble: Making Kin in the Chthulucene*. Durham, NC: Duke University Press.

Hardt, M. (2015). "The Power to Be Affected." *International Journal of Politics, Culture, and Society* 28(3), pp. 215–22.

Hardt, M., and Negri, A. (2000). *Empire*. Cambridge, MA: Harvard University Press.

Harvey, D. (2019). *Marx, Capital and the Madness of Economic Reason*. London: Profile Books.

Hegel, G. W. F. (1977). *Phenomenology of Spirit*. Translated by A. V. Miller. Oxford: Oxford University Press.

Hegel, G. W. F. (2008). *Outlines of the Philosophy of Right*. Translated by T. M. Knox. Oxford: Oxford University Press.

Heidegger, M. (1977). *The Question Concerning Technology and Other Essays*. Translated by W. Lovitt. New York: Garland Publishing.

Helberg, N., Eskens, S., van Drunen, M., Bastian, M., and Moeller, J. (2019). "Implications of AI-Driven Tools in the Media for Freedom of Expression." Institute for Information Law (IViR). Available at: https://rm.coe.int/coe-ai-report-final/168094ce8f

Heyes, C. (2020). "Identity Politics." *Stanford Encyclopedia of Philosophy*. Available at: https://plato.stanford.edu/entries/identity-politics/

Hildebrandt, M. (2015). *Smart Technologies and the End(s) of Law: Novel Entanglements of Law and Technology*. Cheltenham: Edward Elgar Publishing.

Hildreth, R.W. (2009). "Reconstructing Dewey on Power." *Political Theory* 37(6), pp. 780–807.

Hill, K. (2020). "Wrongfully Accused by an Algorithm." *The New York Times*, 24 June.

Hobbes, T. (1996). *Leviathan*. Oxford: Oxford University Press.

Hoffman, M. (2014). *Foucault and Power: The Influence of Political Engagement on Theories of Power*. London: Bloomsbury.

Hughes, J. (2004). *Citizen Cyborg: Why Democratic Societies Must Respond to the Redesigned Human of the Future*. Cambridge, MA: Westview Press.

ILO (International Labour Organization) (2017). *Global Estimates of Modern Slavery*. Geneva: International Labour Office. Available at: https://www.ilo.org/global/publications/books/WCMS_575479/lang--en/index.htm

Israel, T. (2020). *Facial Recognition at a Crossroads: Transformation at our Borders & Beyond*. Ottawa: Samuelson-Glushko Canadian Internet Policy & Public Interest Clinic. Available at: https://cippic.ca/uploads/FR_Transforming_Borders-OVERVIEW.pdf

Javanbakht, A. (2020). "The Matrix Is Already There: Social Media Promised to Connect Us, But Left Us Isolated, Scared, and Tribal." *The Conversation*, November 12. Available at: https://theconversation.com/the-matrix-is-already-here-social-media-promised-to-connect-us-but-left-us-isolated-scared-and-tribal-148799

Jonas, H. (1984). *The Imperative of Responsibility: In Search of an Ethics for the Technological Age*. Chicago: University of Chicago Press.

Kafka, F. (2009). *The Trial*. Translated by M. Mitchell. Oxford: Oxford University Press.

Karppi, T., Kähkönen, L., Mannevuo, M., Pajala, M., and Sihvonen, T. (2016). "Affective Capitalism: Investments and Investigations." *Ephemera: Theory & Politics in Organization* 16(4), pp. 1–13.

Kennedy, H., Steedman, R., and Jones, R. (2020). "Approaching Public Perceptions of Datafication through the Lens of Inequality: A Case Study in Public Service Media." *Information, Communication & Society*. Available at: https://doi.org/10.1080/1369118X.2020.1736122

Kinkead, D., and Douglas, D. M. (2020). "The Network and the Demos: Big Data and the Epistemic Justifications of Democracy." In: K. McNish and J. Gailliott (eds.), *Big Data and Democracy*. Edinburgh: Edinburgh University Press, pp. 119–33.

Kleeman, S. (2015). "Woman Charged with False Reporting after Her Fitbit Contradicted Her Rape Claim." *Mic.com*, June 25. Available at: https://www.mic.com/articles/121319/fitbit-rape-claim

Korinek, A., and Stiglitz, J. (2019). "Artificial Intelligence and Its Implications for Income Distribution and Unemployment." In: A. Agrawal, J. Gans, and A. Goldfarb (eds.), *The Economics of Artificial Intelligence: An Agenda*. Chicago: University of Chicago Press, pp. 349–90.

Kozel, S. (2007). *Closer: Performance, Technologies, Phenomenology.* Cambridge, MA: MIT Press.

Kurzweil, R. (2005). *The Singularity Is Near: When Humans Transcend Biology.* New York: Viking.

Kwet, M. (2019). "Digital Colonialism Is Threatening the Global South." *Al Jazeera*, March 13. Available at: https://www.aljazeera.com/indep th/opinion/digital-colonialism-threatening-global-south-190129140 828809.html

Laclau, E. (2005). *On Populist Reason.* New York: Verso.

Lagerkvist, A. (ed.) (2019). *Digital Existence: Ontology, Ethics and Transcendence in Digital Culture.* Abingdon: Routledge.

Lanier, J. (2010). *You Are Not a Gadget: A Manifesto.* New York: Borzoi Books.

Larson, J., Mattu, S., Kirchner, L., and Angwin, J. (2016). "How We Analyzed the COMPAS Recidivism Algorithm." *ProPublica*, May 23. Available at: https://www.propublica.org/article/how-we-analyzed-the-compas-recidivism-algorithm

Lash, S. (2007). "Power after Hegemony." *Theory, Culture & Society* 24(3), pp. 55–78.

Latour, B. (1993). *We Have Never Been Modern.* Translated by C. Porter. Cambridge, MA: Harvard University Press.

Latour, B. (2004). *Politics of Nature: How to Bring the Sciences into Democracy.* Translated by C. Porter. Cambridge, MA: Harvard University Press.

Lazzarato, M. (1996). "Immaterial Labor." In: P. Virno and M. Hardt (eds.), *Radical Thought in Italy: A Potential Politics.* Minneapolis: University of Minnesota Press, pp. 142–57.

Lazzarato, M. (2014). *Signs and Machines: Capitalism and the Production of Subjectivity.* Translated by J. D. Jordan. Los Angeles: Semiotext(e).

Leopold, A. (1949). *A Sand County Almanac.* New York: Oxford University Press.

Liao, S. M. (ed.) (2020). *Ethics of Artificial Intelligence.* New York: Oxford University Press.

Lin, P., Abney, K., and Jenkins, R. (eds.) (2017). *Robot Ethics 2.0.* New York: Oxford University Press.

Llansó, E. J. (2020). "No Amount of 'AI' in Content Moderation Will Solve Filtering's Prior-Restraint Problem." *Big Data & Society* 7(1). Available at: https://doi.org/10.1177/2053951720920686

Loizidou, E. (2007). *Judith Butler: Ethics, Law, Politics.* New York: Routledge.

Lukes, S. (2019). "Power, Truth and Politics." *Journal of Social Philosophy* 50(4), pp. 562–76.

Lyon, D. (1994). *The Electronic Eye*. Minneapolis: University of Minnesota Press.

Lyon, D. (2014). "Surveillance, Snowden, and Big Data: Capacities, Consequences, Critique." *Big Data & Society* 1(2). Available at: https://doi.org/10.1177/2053951714541861

MacKenzie, A. (2002). *Transductions: Bodies and Machines at Speed*. London: Continuum.

MacKinnon, R., Hickok, E., Bar, A., and Lim, H. (2014). "Fostering Freedom Online: The Role of Internet Intermediaries." Paris: United Nations Educational, Scientific and Cultural Organization (UNESCO). Available at: http://www.unesco.org/new/en/commu nication-and-information/resources/publications-and-communica tion-materials/publications/full-list/fostering-freedom-online-the-role-of-internet-intermediaries/

Magnani, L. (2013). "Abducing Personal Data, Destroying Privacy." In: M. Hildebrandt and K. de Vries (eds.), *Privacy, Due Process, and the Computational Turn*. New York: Routledge, pp. 67–91.

Mann, S., Nolan, J., and Wellman, B. (2002). "Sousveillance: Inventing and Using Wearable Computing Devices for Data Collection in Surveillance Environments." *Surveillance & Society* 1(3), pp. 331–55.

Marcuse, H. (2002). *One-Dimensional Man: Studies in the Ideology of Advanced Industrial Society*. London: Routledge.

Martínez-Bascuñán, M. (2016). "Misgivings on Deliberative Democracy: Revisiting the Deliberative Framework." *World Political Science* 12(2), pp. 195–218.

Marx, K. (1977). *Economic and Philosophic Manuscripts of 1844*. Translated by M. Milligan. Moscow: Progress Publishers.

Marx, K. (1990). *Capital: A Critique of Political Economy*. Vol. 1. Translated by B. Fowkes. London: Penguin.

Massumi, B. (2014). *What Animals Teach Us about Politics*. Durham, NC: Duke University Press.

Matzner, T. (2019). "Plural, Situated Subjects in the Critique of Artificial Intelligence." In: A. Sudmann (ed.), *The Democratization of Artificial Intelligence: Net Politics in the Era of Learning Algorithms*. Bielefeld: Transcript, pp. 109–22.

McCarthy-Jones, S. (2020). "Artificial Intelligence Is a Totalitarian's Dream – Here's How to Take Power Back." *Global Policy*, August 13. Available at: https://www.globalpolicyjournal.com/blog/13/08/2020/artificial-intelligence-totalitarians-dream-heres-how-take-power-back

McDonald, H. P. (2003). "Environmental Ethics and Intrinsic Value." In: H. P. McDonald (ed.), *John Dewey and Environmental Philosophy*. Albany: SUNY Press, pp. 1–56.

McKenzie, J. (2001). *Perform or Else: From Discipline to Performance*. New York: Routledge.

McNay, L. (2008). *Against Recognition*. Cambridge: Polity.

McNay, L. (2010). "Feminism and Post-Identity Politics: The Problem of Agency." *Constellations* 17(4), pp. 512–25.

McQuillan, D. (2019). "The Political Affinities of AI." In: A. Sudmann (ed.), *The Democratization of Artificial Intelligence: Net Politics in the Era of Learning Algorithms*. Bielefeld: Transcript, pp. 163–73.

McStay, A. (2018). *Emotional AI: The Rise of Empathic Media*. London: Sage Publications.

Miessen, M., and Ritts, Z. (eds.) (2019). *Para-Platforms: On the Spatial Politics of Right-Wing Populism*. Berlin: Sternberg Press.

Mill, J. S. (1963). *The Subjection of Women*. In: J. M. Robson (ed.), *Collected Works of John Stuart Mill*. Toronto: Routledge.

Mill, J. S. (1978). *On Liberty*. Indianapolis: Hackett Publishing.

Miller, D. (2003). *Political Philosophy: A Very Short Introduction*. Oxford: Oxford University Press.

Mills, C. W. (1956). *The Power Elite*. New York: Oxford University Press.

Moffitt, B. (2016). *Global Rise of Populism: Performance, Political Style, and Representation*. Stanford: Stanford University Press.

Moore, J. W. (2015). *Capitalism in the Web of Life: Ecology and the Accumulation of Capital*. London: Verso.

Moore, P. (2018). *The Quantified Self in Precarity: Work, Technology and What Counts*. New York: Routledge.

Moravec, H. (1988). *Mind Children: The Future of Robot and Human Intelligence*. Cambridge, MA: Harvard University Press.

Morozov, E. (2013). *To Save Everything, Click Here: Technology, Solutionism, and the Urge to Fix Problems That Don't Exist*. London: Penguin.

Mouffe, C. (1993). *The Return of the Political*. London: Verso.

Mouffe, C. (2000). *The Democratic Paradox*. London: Verso.

Mouffe, C. (2005). *On the Political: Thinking in Action*. London: Routledge.

Mouffe, C. (2016). "Democratic Politics and Conflict: An Agonistic Approach." *Politica Comun* 9. Available at: http://dx.doi.org/10.3998/pc.12322227.0009.011

Murray, D. (2019). *The Madness of the Crowds: Gender, Race and Identity*. London: Bloomsbury.

Næss, A. (1989). *Ecology, Community and Lifestyle: Outline of an Ecosophy*. Edited and translated by D. Rothenberg. Cambridge: Cambridge University Press.

Nemitz, P. F. (2018). "Constitutional Democracy and Technology in the Age of Artificial Intelligence." *SSRN Electronic Journal* 376(2133). Available at: https://doi.org/10.2139/ssrn.3234336

Nguyen, C. T. (2020). "Echo Chambers and Epistemic Bubbles." *Episteme* 17(2), pp. 141–61.

Nielsen, K. (1989). "Marxism and Arguing for Justice." *Social Research* 56(3), pp. 713–39.

Niyazov, S. (2019). "The Real AI Threat to Democracy." *Towards Data Science*, November 15. Available at: https://towardsdatascience.com/democracys-unsettling-future-in-the-age-of-ai-c47b1096746e

Noble, S. U. (2018). *Algorithms of Oppression: How Search Engines Reinforce Racism*. New York: New York University Press.

Nozick, R. (1974). *Anarchy, State, and Utopia*. New York: Basic Books.

Nussbaum, M. (2000). *Women and Human Development: The Capabilities Approach*. Cambridge: Cambridge University Press.

Nussbaum, M. (2006). *Frontiers of Justice: Disability, Nationality, Species Membership*. Cambridge, MA: Harvard University Press.

Nussbaum, M. (2016). *Anger and Forgiveness: Resentment, Generosity, Justice*. New York: Oxford University Press.

Nyholm, S. (2020). *Humans and Robots: Ethics, Agency, and Anthropomorphism*. London: Rowman & Littlefield.

O'Neil, C. (2016). *Weapons of Math Destruction: How Big Data Increases Inequality and Threatens Democracy*. New York: Crown Books.

Ott, K. (2020). "Grounding Claims for Environmental Justice in the Face of Natural Heterogeneities." *Erde* 151(2–3), pp. 90–103.

Owe, A., Baum, S. D., and Coeckelbergh, M. (forthcoming). "How to Handle Nonhumans in the Ethics of Artificial Entities: A Survey of the Intrinsic Valuation of Nonhumans."

Papacharissi, Z. (2011). *A Networked Self: Identity, Community and Culture on Social Network Sites*. New York: Routledge.

Papacharissi, Z. (2015). *Affective Publics: Sentiment, Technology, and Politics*. Oxford: Oxford University Press.

Parikka, J. (2010). *Insect Media: An Archaeology of Animals and Technology*. Minneapolis: University Of Minnesota Press.

Pariser, E. (2011). *The Filter Bubble*. London: Viking.

Parviainen, J. (2010). "Choreographing Resistances: Kinaesthetic Intelligence and Bodily Knowledge as Political Tools in Activist Work." *Mobilities* 5(3), pp. 311–30.

Parviainen, J., and Coeckelbergh, M. (2020). "The Political Choreography of the Sophia Robot: Beyond Robot Rights and Citizenship to Political Performances for the Social Robotics Market." *AI & Society*. Available at: https://doi.org/10.1007/s00146-020-01104-w

Pasquale, F. A. (2019). "Data-Informed Duties in AI Development" 119 Columbia Law Review 1917 (2019), U of Maryland Legal Studies Research Paper No. 2019-14. Available at SSRN: https://ssrn.com/abstract=3503121

Pessach, D., and Shmueli, E. (2020). "Algorithmic Fairness." Available at: https://arxiv.org/abs/2001.09784

Picard, R. W. (1997). *Affective Computing*. Cambridge, MA: MIT Press.

Piketty, T., Saez, E., and Stantcheva, S. (2011). "Taxing the 1%: Why the Top Tax Rate Could Be over 80%." *VOXEU/CEPR*, December 8. Available at: https://voxeu.org/article/taxing-1-why-top-tax-rate-could-be-over-80

Polonski, V. (2017). "How Artificial Intelligence Conquered Democracy." *The Conversation*, August 8. Available at: https://theconversation.com/how-artificial-intelligence-conquered-democracy-77675

Puschmann, C. (2018). "Beyond the Bubble: Assessing the Diversity of Political Search Results." *Digital Journalism* 7(6), pp. 824–43.

Radavoi, C. N. (2020). "The Impact of Artificial Intelligence on Freedom, Rationality, Rule of Law and Democracy: Should We Not Be Debating It?" *Texas Journal on Civil Liberties & Civil Rights* 25(2), pp. 107–29.

Rancière, J. (1991). *The Ignorant Schoolmaster*. Translated by K. Ross. Stanford: Stanford University Press.

Rancière, J. (1999). *Disagreement*. Translated by J. Rose. Minneapolis: University of Minnesota Press.

Rancière, J. (2010). *Dissensus*. Translated by S. Corcoran. New York: Continuum.

Rawls, J. (1971). *A Theory of Justice*. Oxford: Oxford University Press.

Rawls, J. (2001). *Justice as Fairness: A Restatement*. Cambridge, MA: Harvard University Press.

Regan, T. (1983). *The Case for Animal Rights*. Berkeley: University of California Press.

Rensch, A. T.-L. (2019). "The White Working Class Is a Political Fiction." *The Outline*, November 25. Available at: https://theoutline.com/post/8303/white-working-class-political-fiction?zd=1&zi=oggsrqmd

Rhee, J. (2018). *The Robotic Imaginary: The Human and the Price of Dehumanized Labor*. Minneapolis: University of Minnesota Press.

Ricoeur, P. (1978). "The Metaphor Process as Cognition, Imagination, and Feeling." *Critical Inquiry* 5(1), pp. 143–59.

Rieger, S. (2019). "Reduction and Participation." In: A. Sudmann (ed.), *The Democratization of Artificial Intelligence: Net Politics in the Era of Learning Algorithm*. Bielefeld: Transcript, pp. 143–62.

Rivero, N. (2020). "The Pandemic is Automating Emergency Room Triage." *Quartz*, August 21. Available at: https://qz.com/1894714/covid-19-is-boosting-the-use-of-ai-triage-in-emergency-rooms/

Roden, D. (2015). *Posthuman Life: Philosophy at the Edge of the Human*. London: Routledge.

Rolnick, D., Donti, P. L., Kaack, L. H., et al. (2019). "Tackling Climate Change with Machine Learning." Available at: https://arxiv.org/pdf/1906.05433.pdf

Rolston, H. (1988). *Environmental Ethics: Duties to and Values in the Natural World*. Philadelphia: Temple University Press.

Rønnow-Rasmussen, T., and Zimmerman, M. J. (eds.). (2005). *Recent Work on Intrinsic Value*. Dordrecht: Springer Netherlands.

Rousseau, J.-J. (1997). *Of the Social Contract*. In: V. Gourevitch (ed.), *The Social Contract and Other Later Political Writings*. Cambridge: Cambridge University Press, pp. 39–152.

Rouvroy, A. (2013). "The End(s) of Critique: Data-Behaviourism vs. Due-Process." In: M. Hildebrandt and K. de Vries (eds.), *Privacy, Due Process and the Computational Turn: The Philosophy of Law Meets the Philosophy of Technology*. London: Routledge, pp. 143–67.

Rowlands, M. (2009). *Animal Rights: Moral Theory and Practice*. Basingstoke: Palgrave.

Saco, D. (2002). *Cybering Democracy: Public Space and the Internet*. Minneapolis: University of Minnesota Press.

Sætra, H. S. (2020). "A Shallow Defence of a Technocracy of Artificial Intelligence: Examining the Political Harms of Algorithmic Governance in the Domain of Government." *Technology in Society* 62. Available at: https://doi.org/10.1016/j.techsoc.2020.101283.

Sampson, T. D. (2012). *Virality: Contagion Theory in the Age of Networks*. Minneapolis: University of Minnesota Press.

Sandberg, A. (2013). "Morphological Freedom – Why We Not Just Want It, but Need It." In: M. More and M. Vita-More (eds.), *The Transhumanist Reader*. Malden, MA: John Wiley & Sons, pp. 56–64.

Sartori, G. (1987). *The Theory of Democracy Revisited*. Chatham, NJ: Chatham House Publishers.

Sattarov, F. (2019). *Power and Technology*. London: Rowman & Littlefield.

Saurette, P., and Gunster, S. (2011). "Ears Wide Shut: Epistemological Populism, Argutainment and Canadian Conservative Talk Radio." *Canadian Journal of Political Science* 44(1), pp. 195–218.

Scanlon, T. M. (1998). *What We Owe to Each Other*. Cambridge, MA: Harvard University Press.

Segev, E. (2010). *Google and the Digital Divide: The Bias of Online Knowledge*. Oxford: Chandos.

Sharkey, A., and Sharkey, N. (2012). "Granny and the Robots: Ethical issues in Robot Care for the Elderly." *Ethics and Information Technology* 14(1), pp. 27–40.

Simon, F. M. (2019). "'We Power Democracy': Exploring the Promises of the Political Data Analytics Industry." *The Information Society* 35(3), pp. 158–69.

Simonite, T. (2018). "When It Comes to Gorillas, Google Photos

Remains Blind." *Wired*, January 11. Available at: https://www.wired.com/story/when-it-comes-to-gorillas-google-photos-remains-blind/

Singer, P. (2009). *Animal Liberation*. New York: HarperCollins.

Solove, D. J. (2004). *The Digital Person: Technology and Privacy in the Information Age*. New York: New York University Press.

Sparrow, R. (2021). "Virtue and Vice in Our Relationships with Robots." *International Journal of Social Robotics* 13(1), pp. 23–9.

Stark, L., Greene, D., and Hoffmann, A. L. (2021). "Critical Perspectives on Governance Mechanisms for AI/ML Systems." In: J. Roberge and M. Castell (eds.), *The Cultural Life of Machine Learning: An Incursion into Critical AI Studies*. Cham: Palgrave Macmillan, pp. 257–80.

Stiegler, B. (1998). *Technics and Time, 1: The Fault of Epimetheus*. Translated by R. Beardsworth and G. Collins. Stanford: Stanford University Press.

Stiegler, B. (2019). *The Age of Disruption: Technology and Madness in Computational Capitalism*. Translated by D. Ross. Cambridge: Polity.

Stilgoe, J., Owen, R., and Macnaghten, P. (2013). "Developing A Framework for Responsible Innovation." *Research Policy* 42(9), pp. 1568–80.

Strubell, E., Ganesh, A., and McCallum, A. (2019). "Energy and Policy Considerations for Deep Learning in NLP." Available at: https://arxiv.org/abs/1906.02243

Suarez-Villa, L. (2009). *Technocapitalism: A Critical Perspective on Technological Innovation and Corporatism*. Philadelphia: Temple University Press.

Sudmann, A. (ed.) (2019). *The Democratization of Artificial Intelligence: Net Politics in the Era of Learning Algorithms*. Bielefeld: Transcript.

Sun, T., Gaut, A., Tang, S., Huang, Y., El Shereif, M., Zhao, J., Mirza, D., Belding, E., Chang, K.-W., and Wang, W. Y. (2019). "Mitigating Gender Bias in Natural Language Processing: Literature Review." In: A. Korhonen, D. Traum, and L. Marquez (eds.), *Proceedings of the 57th Annual Meeting of the Association of Computational Linguistics*, pp. 1630–40. Available at: https://www.aclweb.org/anthology/P19-1159.pdf

Sun, X., Wang, N., Chen, C.-y., Ni, J.-m., Agrawal, A., Cui, X., Venkataramani, S., El Maghraoui, K., Srinivasan, V. (2020). "Ultra-Low Precision 4-Bit Training of Deep Neutral Networks." In: H. Larochelle, M. Ranzato, R. Hadsell, M. F. Balcan, and H. Lin (eds.), *Advances in Neural Information Processing Systems 33 Pre-Proceedings*. Proceedings of the 34th Conference on Neutral Information Processing Systems (NeurIPS 2020), Vancouver, Canada. Available at: https://proceedings.neurips.cc/paper/2020/file/13b919438259814cd5be8cb45877d577-Paper.pdf

Sunstein, C. R. (2001). *Republic.com*. Princeton: Princeton University Press.

Susser, D., Roessler, B., and Nissenbaum, H. (2019). "Technology, Autonomy, and Manipulation." *Internet Policy Review* 8(2). https://doi.org/10.14763/2019.2.1410

Swift, A. (2019). *Political Philosophy*. Cambridge: Polity.

Tangerman, V. (2019). "Amazon Used an AI to Automatically Fire Low-Productivity Workers." *Futurism*, April 26. Available at: https://futurism.com/amazon-ai-fire-workers

Thaler, R. H., and Sunstein, C. R. (2009). *Nudge: Improving Decisions about Health, Wealth, and Happiness*. Revised edition. London: Penguin.

Thompson, N., Harari, Y. N., and Harris, T. (2018). "When Tech Knows You Better Than You Know Yourself." *Wired*, April 10. Available at: https://www.wired.com/story/artificial-intelligence-yuval-noah-harari-tristan-harris/

Thorseth, M. (2008). "Reflective Judgement and Enlarged Thinking Online." *Ethics and Information Technology* 10, pp. 221–31.

Titley, G. (2020). *Is Free Speech Racist?* Cambridge: Polity.

Tocqueville, A. (2000). *Democracy in America*. Translated by H. C. Mansfield and D. Winthrop. Chicago: University of Chicago Press.

Tolbert, C. J., McNeal, R. S., and Smith, D. A. (2003). "Enhancing Civic Engagement: The Effect of Direct Democracy on Political Participation and Knowledge." *State Politics and Policy Quarterly* 3(1), pp. 23–41.

Tschakert, P. (2020). "More-Than-Human Solidarity and Multispecies Justice in the Climate Crisis." *Environmental Politics*. Available at: https://doi.org/10.1080/09644016.2020.1853448

Tufekci, Z. (2018)."Youtube, the Great Radicalizer." *The New York Times*, March 10.

Turkle, S. (2011). *Alone Together: Why We Expect More from Technology and Less from Each Other*. New York: Basic Books.

Umbrello, S., and Sorgner, S. (2019). "Nonconscious Cognitive Suffering: Considering Suffering Risks of Embodied Artificial Intelligence." *Philosophies* 4(2). Available at: https://doi.org/10.3390/philosophies4020024

UN (United Nations) (1948). *Universal Declaration of Human Rights*. Available at: https://www.un.org/en/about-us/universal-declaration-of-human-rights

UN (United Nations) (2018). "Promotion and Protection of the Right to Freedom of Opinion and Expression." Seventy-third session, August 29. Available at: https://www.undocs.org/A/73/348

UNICRI (United Nations International Crime and Justice Research Institute) and INTERPOL (International Criminal Police

Organization) (2019). *Artificial Intelligence and Robotics for Law Enforcement*. Turin and Lyon: UNICRI and INTERPOL. Available at: https://www.europarl.europa.eu/cmsdata/196207/UNICRI%20-%20Artificial%20intelligence%20and%20robotics%20for%20law%20enforcement.pdf

Vallor, S. (2016). *Technology and the Virtues*. New York: Oxford University Press.

van den Hoven, J. (2013). "Value Sensitive Design and Responsible Innovation." In: R. Owen, J. Bessant, and M. Heintz (eds.), *Responsible Innovation: Managing the Responsible Emergence of Science and Innovation in Society*. London: Wiley, pp. 75–83.

van Dijk, J. (2020). *The Network Society*. Fourth edition. London: Sage Publications.

Van Parijs, P. (1995). *Real Freedom for All*. Oxford: Clarendon Press.

Varela, F., Thompson, E. T., and Rosch, E. (1991). *The Embodied Mind: Cognitive Science and Human Experience*. Cambridge, MA: MIT Press.

Véliz, C. (2020). *Privacy Is Power: Why and How You Should Take Back Control of Your Data*. London: Bantam Press.

Verbeek, P.-P. (2005). *What Things Do: Philosophical Reflections on Technology, Agency, and Design*. University Park: Pennsylvania State University Press.

Vidal, J. (2011). "Bolivia Enshrines Natural World's Rights with Equal Status for Mother Earth." *The Guardian*, April 10. Available at: https://www.theguardian.com/environment/2011/apr/10/bolivia-enshrines-natural-worlds-rights

von Schomberg, R. (ed.) (2011). *Towards Responsible Research and Innovation in the Information and Communication Technologies and Security Technologies Fields*. Luxembourg: Publication Office of the European Union. Available at: https://op.europa.eu/en/publication-detail/-/publication/60153e8a-0fe9-4911-a7f4-1b530967ef10

Wahl-Jorgensen, K. (2008). "Theory Review: On the Public Sphere, Deliberation, Journalism and Dignity." *Journalism Studies* 9(6), pp. 962–70.

Walk Free Foundation. (2018). *The Global Slavery Index*. Available at: https://www.globalslaveryindex.org/resources/downloads/

Wallach, W., and Allen, C. (2009). *Moral Machines*. New York: Oxford University Press.

Warburton, N. (2009). *Free Speech: A Very Short Introduction*. Oxford: Oxford University Press.

Webb, A. (2019). *The Big Nine: How the Tech Titans and Their Thinking Machines Could Warp Humanity*. New York: Hachette Book Group.

Webb, M. (2020). *Coding Democracy: How Hackers Are Disrupting Power, Surveillance, and Authoritarianism.* Cambridge, MA: MIT Press.

Westlund, A. (2009). "Rethinking Relational Autonomy." *Hypatia* 24(4), pp. 26–49.

Winner, L. (1980). "Do Artifacts Have Politics?" *Daedalus* 109(1), pp. 121–36.

Winner, L. (1986). *The Whale and the Reactor.* Chicago: University of Chicago Press.

Wolfe, C. (2010). *What Is Posthumanism?* Minneapolis: University of Minnesota Press.

Wolfe, C. (2013). *Before the Law: Humans and Other Animals in a Biopolitical Frame.* Chicago: University of Chicago Press.

Wolfe, C. (2017). "Posthumanism Thinks the Political: A Genealogy of Foucault's *The Birth of Biopolitics.*" *Journal of Posthuman Studies* 1(2), pp. 117–35.

Wolff, J. (2016). *An Introduction to Political Philosophy.* Third edition. Oxford: Oxford University Press.

Yeung, K. (2016). "'Hypernudge': Big Data as a Mode of Regulation by Design." *Information, Communication & Society* 20(1), pp. 118–36.

Young, I. (2000). *Inclusion and Democracy.* Oxford: Oxford University Press.

Zimmermann, A., Di Rosa, E., and Kim, H. (2020). "Technology Can't Fix Algorithmic Injustice." *Boston Review*, January 9. Available at: http://bostonreview.net/science-nature-politics/annette-zimmer mann-elena-di-rosa-hochan-kim-technology-cant-fix-algorithmic

Zolkos, M. (2018). "Life as a Political Problem: The Post-Human Turn in Political Theory." *Political Studies Review* 16(3), pp. 192–204.

Zuboff, S. (2015). "Big Other: Surveillance Capitalism and the Prospects of an Information Civilization." *Journal of Information Technology* 30(1), pp. 75–89.

Zuboff, S. (2019). *The Age of Surveillance Capitalism: The Fight for a Human Future at the New Frontier of Power.* London: Profile Books.

Index